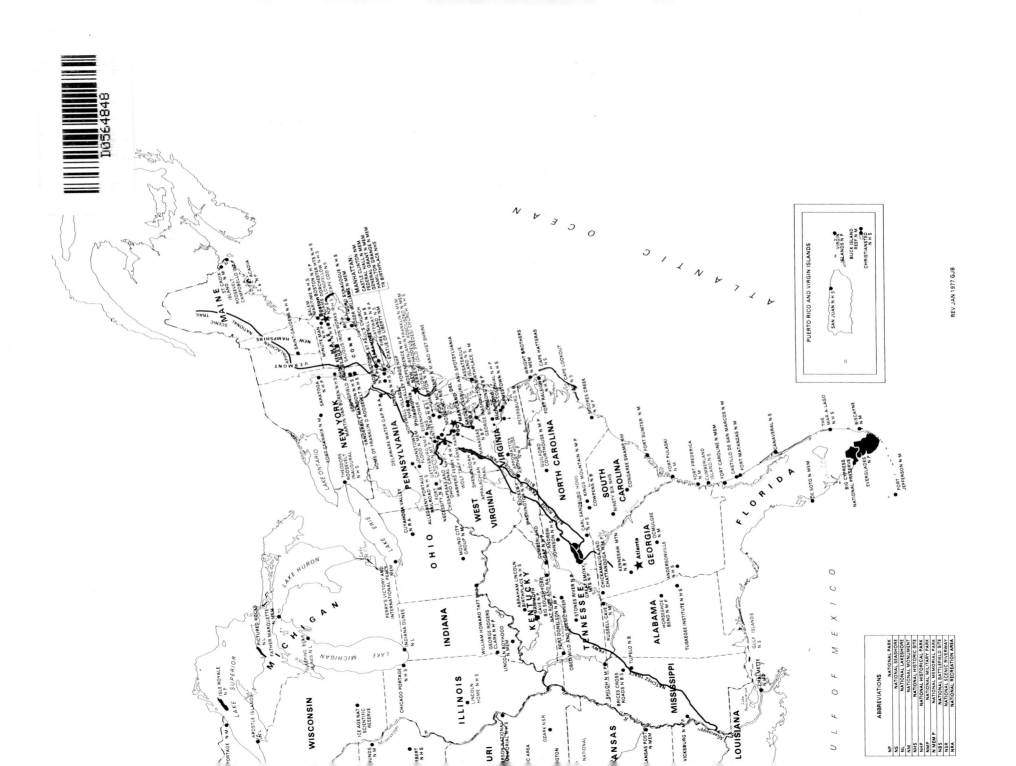

II

Your National Park System
in the *Southwest*
in words and color

Earl Jackson

SOUTHWEST PARKS AND
MONUMENTS ASSOCIATION

Box 1562, Globe, Arizona 85501

III

Library of Congress Catalog Card Number: 67-26925
Standard Book Number: 0-911408-50-9

Fourth Printing (Revised) 1978

Popular series No. 11

Published in cooperation with
the National Park Service

Printed in the United States of America

IV

Foreword

Something unusual keeps this book from *being just another* partial glance at the National Parks. For one thing, it describes and illustrates, in color, each National Park Service unit in the Southwest *open for public use*. For another, every area description has been written by a National Park Service employee or, in many cases, the author, who grew up in the Service and served in, or worked for it, during most of 50 years. Last but not least, each article was first submitted in draft form to the official in charge of the area for criticism and correction, before going into print. With each reprint all information is similarly updated. This makes the book, its area maps and "How to Get There" portion as accurate as humanly possible.

Acknowledgements

Many persons helped produce this book as a cooperative effort between Southwest Parks and Monuments Association and the National Park Service. Park people went to great effort to provide good color illustrations, sometimes with government-owned pictures, sometimes with loan of their own transparencies and sometimes with borrowed transparencies from friends of the Park Service. Special recognition is due our Board of Directors, which foresaw the original need for the book and assigned me the pleasure of producing it. Last but not least was the competent help provided by Associate Editor Carolyn Dodson. Any errors are mine; any merits, those of many.

— Earl Jackson

Photo Courtesy Credits (No specific credit for most National Park Service views): . . . . Cover — Dwight L. Hamilton . . . . . Frontispiece — Allen R. Hagood . . . . Alibates — Mrs. Charles Barkley . . . . . Bent's Old Fort — Morris S. Jordan . . . . . Carlsbad Caverns — Cavern Supply Company . . . . . Casa Grande Ruins — Petley Studios . . . Chaco Canyon — Douglas B. Anderson . . . . . Fort Larned — Jake E. Tothero . . . . Hovenweep — Jon Harman . . . Organ Pipe Cactus — Earl E. Petroff . . . . . Rainbow Bridge — Art Kidwell . . . . Rocky Mountain — Dwight L. Hamilton . . . . Sunset Crater — Petley Studios . . . . Wupatki — Richard V. Harris . . . . . Zion — Allen R. Hagood.

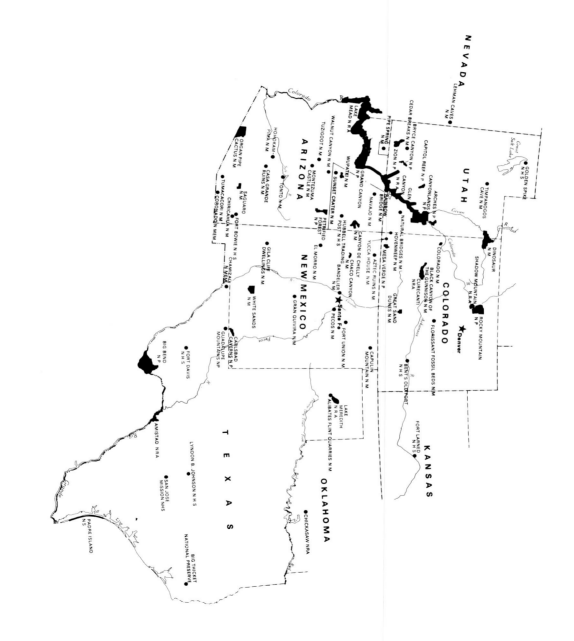

NATIONAL PARK SYSTEM
SOUTHWESTERN UNITED STATES
1977

VI

Table of Contents

ILLUSTRATIONS

Alibates
TEXAS

Alibates flint was one of the most distinctive stones used by early nomadic hunters of the High Plains. Its multitude of bright colors, in endless variations and patterns, made it easily identifiable in contrast with the one characteristic shade of most flints. Hard to flake, but holding an edge very well, it was fashioned into an amazing variety of everyday "survival" tools, and was a medium of trade in many Great Plains and Southwestern areas.

There is evidence, from 10,000 B.C. to possibly as late as the 1870's, for almost continuous use of Alibates flint (agatized dolomite) during 12,000 years. Ancient men, no doubt women also, dug with hands and sticks through the thin soil of a ridge to reach unweathered flint. Around their shallow quarry pits are chunks and pieces of the material, waste tailings from quarrying operations. Choice pieces were chipped and flaked by early toolmakers into knives, hammers, chisels, drills, axes, awls, fishhooks, buttons, hoes, and scrapers, as well as dart points and arrowheads. Chip strewn sites of these early craftsmen have been found on bluffs along the Canadian River of the Texas Panhandle.

In late prehistoric times, from about A.D. 1200 to 1450, we note a change from nomadic hunters who followed the game trails and lived in temporary homes. During this period some people settled permanently near the quarries and became dry farmers. We refer to them as the Panhandle Pueblo Culture, because they were Plains Village Indians whose homes revealed influence of Southwestern pueblo style architecture. This is not too surprising, for they were traders as well as

farmers, trading flint and buffalo products to Pueblo Indians of the Southwest for Pacific Coast seashells, obsidian, turquoise, and painted pottery, and they picked up construction ideas as well.

The famous flint comes from a 26 square kilometer* (10 square miles) area around Lake Meredith, on the Canadian River. It occurs in a layer up to 1.8 meters (6 feet) thick, usually just below ground surface. What does "Alibates" mean? It is derived from an early cowboy, Allie Bates, who lived in a cabin near the ruins of one of the pueblo type villages.

Alibates National Monument is open to the public on a limited basis. Your visit should begin at the Bates Canyon Information Station of Lake Meredith Recreation Area (formerly Sanford Recreation Area). Although Alibates as a park is undeveloped you may visit the quarry pits on guided walking tours, limited to no more than 20 persons each. These tours are conducted by park rangers daily from Memorial Day thru Labor Day. Off-season tours are arranged on request by writing to: Superintendent, Lake Meredith Recreation Area, P.O. Box 1438, Fritch, Texas 79036. You may also see exhibits of archeological material from the region, and a conjecture of a Panhandle Pueblo structure, at the Panhandle Plains Historical Museum, West Texas State University, in Canyon, Texas 26 kilometers (16 miles) south of Amarillo.

*Yes, we're helping introduce Americans to the metric system of measurements, to make interpretation more meaningful for park visitors from other nations.

1

Amistad

TEXAS

The Amistad Recreation Area is located about midway along the Rio Grande boundary between Texas and Coahuila, Mexico. The reservoir project began in 1963, and the dam was completed early in 1969. It is called the Amistad (Friendship) Reservoir, and aids flood control and water conservation. There are plans for possible use for generating hydroelectric power.

The dam has a concrete-gravity section in the river channel, with flanking earth embankments. It is 77 m (254 feet) high from riverbed level and impounds a maximum of over 5½ million acre feet of water. At typical operating pool levels, the lake extends through more than 112 km (70 miles) of low, rolling hill country and shallow open valleys with bluffs and high cliff sections up the Rio Grande; 40 km (25 miles) up the Devil's River (joining the Rio Grande just above the dam site); and 22 km (14 miles) up the Pecos River. The total shoreline is nearly 1,609 km (1,000 miles) long. Total surface area of the lake is 27,135 ha (67,000 acres); 17,516 ha (43,250 acres) of the total are in the United States.

The reservoir furnishes various types of water recreation from fishing and boating through excellent SCUBA diving due to unusual clarity of the water.

The semi-arid climate, about 38 cm (15 inches) annual rainfall, is marked by hot summers and mild winters, with only occasional frost. Altitude ranges from about 305 to 458 m (1,000 to 1,500 feet) above sea level.

Three different developed sites along the American shore have complete marina facilities, and there are nine other public boat launching sites at various places as well as a large public swim beach. Across the dam on the Mexican side is a recreation area with tables, ramadas and children's playground equipment, as well as a small restaurant. A short distance farther up the shore is a marina and public boat launching ramp.

The region has an interesting history and prehistory. Evidence of human occupation goes back nearly 14,000 years. Over 250 archeological sites, now mostly under water in the reservoir area, contained artifacts in rock shelters, caves and terrace sites. Colorful petroglyphs and pictographs were found in many rock shelters. Some excavated sites in Seminole Canyon near U.S. Highway 90 will be used as inplace interpretive exhibits by the Texas State Parks who own this land. Spanish exploration here dates from the year 1590.

The area is bounded by some of the huge "working ranches" of Texas, punctuated by historic towns and remains of military posts and camps of the early west.

Plant and animal life is characteristic of three geographical areas, the Chihuahuan Desert, limestone uplands of the Edwards Plateau, and the Gulf Coastal Plain. Here occur the lechuguilla, beargrass, catclaw, ocotillo, yucca, ceniza, sotol, mescalbean, creosotebush, leatherplant, and various cactus species. Few trees occur, except on flood plains of permanent streams. Wildlife includes ringtails, peccaries, armadillos, whitetail deer, and rock squirrels.

Unusual animals found (or expected) include: Mexican opossum, coati, ocelot, tropical indigo snake, South Texas ground snake, Texas alligator lizard, golden-fronted woodpecker, and boat-tailed grackle.

Certain areas are designated for hunting doves, quail and waterfowl in season as well as bow hunting for deer. State and Federal laws apply. Check at Park Headquarters for hunt area maps and special regulations.

Amistad Recreation Area is managed by the National Park Service through agreement with the International Boundary and Water Commission. The superintendent lives in nearby Del Rio. His mailing address is P.O. Box 1463, Del Rio, Texas 78840.

2

Arches
UTAH

On the edge of the Colorado Plateau, at the gateway to the fabulous canyonlands country, lies Arches National Park, a natural rock garden of sculptured art. Established as a National Monument in 1929, it became a 286 sq km (110 square mile) National Park in 1972. Here are more natural stone arches, windows, spires and pinnacles than anywhere else in the nation. Formed by erosion from a 91 m (300-foot) layer of buff-colored sedimentary rock called Entrada Sandstone are spectacular towers, sweeping coves, shapes resembling men and animals, balanced rocks, and arches.

Probably the best known of the arches is Delicate Arch. Rising in solitary majesty 26 m (85 feet) above a "slickrock" bowl, it spans 20 m (65 feet). Landscape Arch, from an engineering as well as a scenic standpoint, is most amazing. Believed to be the world's longest natural stone span, it is 89 m (291 feet) long, weighs many tons, and at one point is only 1.8 m (6 feet) thick! And there are scores of others, each distinctly spectacular.

What formed these wonders? Wind, rain, ice, and sun were Nature's tools. First the wind deposited a thick layer of sand which hardened into sandstone; then the rock was split into thousands of vertical and horizontal parallel cracks. The combined forces of wind, water, and alternate freezing and thawing widened and deepened the cracks until they were deep, vertical-walled canyons, separated by thin rock slabs, or fins. Dissolving action of water followed horizontal cracks in the fins, and with the aid of gravity caused great blocks to become loose and fall away, perforating the fins with holes. Further weathering enlarged the holes, and sand-laden wind smoothed away rough edges, forming the windows and arches. This process still continues with new arches and other weird shapes being formed as old ones collapse:

Here are great stone cities of towering skyscrapers, a parade of stone elephants, three gossips, and Adam and Eve in their stone Garden of Eden. Viewing the Fiery Furnace near the Devil's Garden in the setting sun, we can imagine red flames licking the sky.

Arches lies between 1,281 and 1,708 m (4,200 and 5,600 feet) elevation, and averages 24 cm (9.5 inches) of rainfall per year. The many birds, mammals, reptiles, and plants which live here must adapt to temperatures normally ranging from winter low of about −9.4 C (15° Fahrenheit) to summer high of 38 to 65 C (100 to 105° F.).

At the visitor center are exhibits that explain the natural history of the area, and a uniformed employee is on duty there to help plan your visit for maximum enjoyment. Paved or graded roads make many of the area's features accessible by car. Hiking trails lead you to others, and, as is generally true everywhere, yield much that is missed by motorists.

No food or lodging facilities occur in the Park, but restaurants, motels, hotels and commercial campgrounds are located in Moab, only 8 km (5 miles) from the entrance. The superintendent of Canyonlands National Park is also in charge of Arches, and his address is: 446 South Main, Moab, Utah 84532.

3

Aztec Ruins
NEW MEXICO

One of the largest pre-Spanish towns in the Southwest is located in the 11 ha (27-acre) Aztec Ruins National Monument (established in 1923) near the beautiful Animas River of northwestern New Mexico. The largest of several buildings here was a 3-story communal dwelling (pueblo) of 500 rooms, surrounding a central plaza containing a huge kiva (ceremonial lodge). Early U.S. settlers in the region erroneously assumed the ancient builders were Aztecs, hence the name of the ruins and of the modern town of Aztec.

Pueblo Indians developed a culture well adapted to the environment of the San Juan River drainage, from its Colorado and New Mexico sources to its great bends in Utah. As early as A.D. 500, they settled in small villages and grew corn and squash, adding beans to their crops in the 700's. The introduction of new architectural techniques permitted new types of construction and larger pueblos. By A.D. 1100 artisans of this period produced finely worked tools of stone, bone, and wood as well as beautifully decorated pottery and intricately woven cotton cloth. Their livelihood, as in earlier days, still depended primarily on agriculture. Crops were supplemented by wild plant foods in season, and wild game.

The concentration of people at Aztec Ruins resulted in an urban-like development, implying a social organization of some complexity. Countless tons of dressed sandstone buildings blocks were hauled from quarries up to 6 km (4 miles) away, without benefit of metal, wheels, or beasts of burden. In a short span of time, large numbers of multi-storied houses were constructed, with a preconceived community plan in mind. A variety of small kivas and a central great kiva also suggest an involved ceremonial complex.

A focal point of high culture in the San Juan basin until the mid 1100's, having great influence on the people at Aztec Ruins, was Chaco Canyon, 105 km (65 miles) south. After the middle of that century Chaco's influence declined, to be gradually superseded by that of Mesa Verde to the north. By A.D. 1200, Mesa Verde ideas dominated the San Juan Region. Aztec, between these famous centers, was influenced by both, and the successions of influence are interestingly revealed in their art and architecture. By A.D. 1300, the entire basin was abandoned, partly due to the severe droughts of 1276-1299.

Ruins of this vicinity first appeared in history on the Miera y Pacheco map of 1776-77 and were well described by Prof. J. S. Newberry in 1859. Nearby modern settlement started in 1876. Two years later scientific investigation of the ruins began under Earl H. Morris of the American Museum of Natural History. He excavated much of the large ruin between 1916 and 1921, and in 1934 completely restored the Great Kiva. Kivas of this type, representing the peak of Pueblo religious architecture centuries ago, are not used by modern Pueblo people.

Aztec Ruins National Monument is on an all-weather highway. There are no overnight camping facilities in the Monument, although a variety of overnight accommodations and other services are offered in nearby towns. Open year round, it has a pueblo-style visitor center and a series of indoor and outdoor exhibits. The museum and self-guiding ruins trail help you understand the archeological story, and guided tours are provided for large groups upon request. Address inquiries to the superintendent at P.O. Box U, Aztec, New Mexico 87410.

Bandelier
NEW MEXICO

The rim of the Valle Grande, one of the world's largest calderas (collapsed volcanoes), forms the Jemez Mountains of north-central New Mexico. On the southeast flank of the mountains lies the 120 sq km (46 square mile) Bandelier National Monument, established in 1916.

The mountains are composed of consolidated volcanic ash (tuff) and basaltic lava from the old volcano. Their southeast flank has been cut by streams that have carved sheer-walled canyons as they flowed to the nearby Rio Grande.

Many different types of Indian ruins, resulting from a mass influx of people in the late 1200's, dot the area. Small compact dwellings, large circular pueblos with central plazas, cavate dwellings, isolated kivas, seasonal farm sites, ceremonial caves, and shrines were all constructed on and adapted to a variety of sites in rugged locales of this canyon-mesa country.

The most accessible ruins are in Frijoles Canyon, where village remains extend for 3.2 km (2 miles). Masonry houses were built four stories high against the cliff, and behind them caves were dug into the soft but consolidated ash. Tyuonyi, a large multistoried, circular pueblo on the canyon floor, had about 400 rooms. Some of the canyon structures may have been still occupied when Coronado visited the region in 1540, but his expedition left no specific reference to towns of this area.

These farming people grew beans (frijoles), corn, and squash, hunted native plant foods and wild game, wove turkey feather blankets and possibly cotton cloth, and made glaze-decorated pottery. Exact reasons for abandonment of their pueblos aren't known, although the drought of the late 1500's may have been the major factor. Some of their descendents live today in Rio Grande pueblos.

Tsankawi, a detached section of the Monument, has a large, unexcavated, mesa-top pueblo ruin, accessible by a partly original 3.2 km (2-mile) self-guiding trail. Walking time: about 1½ hours.

Considerable variation in terrain and elevation from the Rio Grande to the Valle Grande creates an interesting diversity of plant and animal life. Three life zones occur in Bandelier: the Upper Sonoran Zone of pinyon and juniper by the river, the Transition Zone of ponderosa pines on the higher mesas, and highest of all, the Canadian Zone of spruce, fir, and aspen.

Most of Bandelier is wilderness area, accessible only by trails, of which more than 97 km (60 miles) are maintained, leading to Alamo Canyon, the Stone Lions, Painted Cave, pueblo ruins of San Miguel and Yapashi, and White Rock Canyon. Especially popular is the hike from Upper Frijoles Crossing downstream to Monument headquarters, where you should register for all proposed back country hikes, obtaining wilderness permits when required. This is for your safety and may prevent needless search.

Visitor center exhibits tell of human occupancy in the region, and slide programs aid orientation and understanding. In summer, guided walking tours and evening campfire talks widen your acquaintance with archeology, ethnology, and natural history. The principal ruins in Frijoles Canyon are accessible by trail, with self-guiding booklets.

The Monument is open year round (visitor center closed Dec. 25). From May to September, temperatures range from about 10 C (50 F) at night to 27 C (80 F) in daytime, with thunderstorms in July and August. Relative humidity is generally low.

The Juniper campground on the mesa near the entrance station has tent space, table, and fireplace for each site. There are modern restrooms, water taps, and trailer sites. A lunch area is in the canyon near the visitor center.

Frijoles Canyon Lodge, open in summer, provides a snack bar, a curio shop, and campers' supplies. Mail address is Los Alamos, New Mexico 87544. The superintendent in charge of the Monument has the same address.

5

Bent's Old Fort

COLORADO

Bent's Old Fort National Historic Site was established and added to the National Park system in 1961. The fort was the principal outpost of American civilization on the Southeastern plains between 1833 and 1849. Charles Bent, William Bent and Ceran St. Vrain formed a business partnership in 1830 to exploit the profitable Santa Fe trade with Mexico as well as fur and buffalo robe trading with the Indians. To this end a large enclosed fort was constructed near the banks of the Arkansas River. It was constructed of adobe bricks and timber. In time it would have 41 rooms and other areas of use.

The fort is situated on the mountain route of the Santa Fe Trail well within bison country and the crossroads of five different Indian tribes. The Bent's and St. Vrain for 16 years managed a private trading empire stretching from Texas into Wyoming, from the Rockies to middle Kansas. They also had large mercantile stores in Taos and Santa Fe. From St. Louis caravans brought wagonloads of beads, cloth, guns and other items prized by the Indians to the fort for trade. From Mexico, Charles Bent and St. Vrain sent horses, blankets, grain and various items obtained by barter at the stores that the company owned. Within a few years Bent, St. Vrain and Company had built up a profitable business.

With the annexation of Texas by the United States in 1845, Mexico viewed the act as one of war. With the approach of armed conflict, the United States designated the adobe trading post as the advance base for invasion of New Mexico by Gen. Stephen Watts, Kearny's Army of the West.

The steady flow of soldiers across the plains during the Mexican War, with settlers, goldseekers, and adventurers that came later, constituted a white tide that irrevocably changed the Great Plains. The company was caught between the millstones of resentful Indians and invading whites. Indian warfare commenced seriously in 1847, and from then on the days of rich trading were gone.

Charles Bent, appointed governor of the newly won territory of New Mexico, was killed in 1847 during a revolt in Taos. This blow, together with the sharp decline in business, destroyed the firm. William Bent set fire to the storerooms and abandoned the fort in 1849. What had been the center of a giant commercial empire was left a smoldering monument to Manifest Destiny.

The National Park Service has recently reconstructed and refurnished Bent's Old Fort as it would have appeared in 1846. Visitors can tour the fort and enjoy a special film presentation concerning its history. From the parking lot, it is a short walk along the path to the reconstructed fort. There are no overnight camping facilities at the park. Address of the resident superintendent is Box 581, La Junta, Colorado 81050.

Big Bend
TEXAS

This immense Chihuahuan Desert wilderness, more like parts of Mexico than the United States, is only separated from Mexico by 172 km (107 miles) of the Rio Grande and some 458 m (1,500 foot) deep canyons cut by the River. You can motor within easy walking distance of two of these canyon sections, Santa Elena on the west and Boquillas Canyon on the southeast side.

The Park is the home of the giant dagger yucca and the lechuguilla agave and about 1,100 other plant species, including the lovely strawberry cactus. Wildlife is abundant, and you have a chance to see the peccary, the mule deer, the gray fox, the coyote, and the kit fox, and occasionally the mountain lion is observed crossing roads and trails.

The Park and all its concessions, services, cabins, meals, service stations, saddle horses, etc., operate the year around. You have a choice in altitude from 549 m (1,800 feet) in river areas to 1647 m (5,400 feet) in Chisos Basin (the Basin), nestled in the rugged Chisos Mountains which rise to 2390 m (7,835 feet) at Emory Peak. The South Rim horse trail in the Chisos reaches 2196 m (7,200 feet) and the highest point reached by auto is 1769 m (5,800 feet) in Panther Pass where you enter the Basin.

Three paved roads approach Big Bend. Most roads in the Park are paved, and are normally in good condition, but may be impassable immediately after rainstorms.

The Rio Grande Village campground is ideal for winter, rather hot in summer; the one at Chisos Basin is ideal for summer, with nights cool, sometimes windy, and occasionally freezing in winter.

Regular campground space cannot be reserved, although space in group camping areas can; for them, advance reservations are advised. Trailers are permitted in all campgrounds, but there are no sewer, water, or electrical connections; steep grades and sharp curves make access to Chisos Basin difficult for many trailers, and impossible for some of the larger ones. Check with a park ranger before taking a trailer into the Basin. Trailer facilities, concession operated, with water, sewer, and electrical hook-ups are available at Panther Junction and Rio Grande Village.

Park Headquarters at Panther Junction has an information office, and is an ideal location for getting oriented and planning motor, hiking, or horseback trips.

The Basin has cabin and lunchroom facilities. Cabin reservations should be made as far ahead as possible during heavy travel from April through September and for all holiday weekends. The day-long horseback trip to the South Rim of the Chisos is a memorable one, and shorter horse trips are available from the Chisos Remuda, operating in the Basin.

Evening programs are offered in the Basin at the campfire circle by Park Naturalists during the summer season, and in winter season at Rio Grande Village. Self-guiding foot trails, both for "easy" rambles and for vigorous hikes, are available, and are well worth taking. Remember, however, there are no doctors or nurses in the Park, and you should carry water and first aid equipment.

For further information, contact the superintendent at Big Bend National Park, Texas 79834.

Big Thicket
TEXAS

"You can find anything in there," old settlers used to say, "from a cricket to an elephant." Trying to separate fact from fiction, conservationists have long maintained that the Big Thicket is unique. Viewed from the air, some of the country looks like jungle; lush, dense, gnarled, with tannin colored water glistening in the sun between tree overhangs. Vines cling to treetops, birds sun on dead branches, and flowering tree blossoms blaze white against dark green. But from the air the real diversity is hidden. One needs to get on the ground to see that the Big Thicket is a biological crossroad featuring both temperate and subtropical plants and animals, along with species from the dry west. Where else will you find roadrunners alongside cottonmouths, yucca alongside cypress, and orchids near cacti?

Big Thicket National Preserve, just north of Beaumont, Texas, was established in 1974 and exemplifies representative fragments of the "Big Thicket" which once covered approximately 1,417,500 ha (3½ million acres) of East Texas. This vast area of diversity was and is being reduced through farming, timber, oil exploration, and residential needs of man. Today, just 34,242 ha (84,550 acres) of this diversity is being preserved in 12 disjunct representative Preserve units and river corridors. It is the first National Park Service area to be designated a "National Preserve." This new concept affords a multiplicity of uses while retaining the traditional concept of N.P.S. administration.

The Preserve is still in the land acquisition stage and it is hoped some units will be opened to visitors in 1978. Once open, visitors will be able to park and visit the units on trails. In the future, portions of certain units will be accessible by shuttle bus system.

Visitors will eventually be able to see part of the "Big Thicket" diversity, especially remnant examples of mature pine-hardwood forests, closed canopy wilderness examples of Upper and Lower "Big Thicket," and stream bottom and flood plain vegetative associations.

Along with diversity in vegetation comes a variety of wildlife. The secluded character of much of the remaining Big Thicket makes it excellent habitat for many forms of wildlife. Overwintering birds find the Preserve a haven and it has been said that over 300 species reside in or pass through the area.

In addition to wilderness qualities in many units, the preserve has several corridor units offering opportunities for canoeists and fishermen.

Those interested in history will find century-old mores and folkways altered little by modernity, and many individuals cling tenaciously to their fathers' heritage. When the "Big Thicket" area was under Spain's control, Europeans came into contact with indigenous Indians who eventually became extinct because of European disease. The Alabama and Coushatta Indians immigrated to the area and have resided on a reservation adjacent to one of the park's units for over 100 years.

Big Thicket National Preserve is unique and offers people in large nearby cities an opportunity to get away from the rush and noise of everyday life and enjoy relative quiet and solitude in a setting once enjoyed by their forefathers.

For further information write: Superintendent, Big Thicket National Preserve, P.O. Box 7408, Beaumont, TX 77706.

Black Canyon of the Gunnison
COLORADO

You feel pretty small, standing on the rim of the chasm, as you hear the roar of the Gunnison River, 610 m (2,000 feet) below. No other canyon in North America combines the depth, narrowness, sheerness, and brooding appearance of this one.

Although the gorge cuts through 85 km (53 miles) of southwestern Colorado, only the deepest and most spectacular 19 km (12 miles) lie within the National Monument, established in 1933 and now embracing over 52 sq km (20 square miles) of rugged country. Slanting rays of sunlight penetrate between the heavily shadowed dark gray walls for brief periods in the day, hence the logic of the name. Canyon depths range from 528 m (1730 feet) to 823 m (2700 feet) and at the Narrows it is only 396 m (1300 feet) wide at the rim and as little as 12 m (40 feet) at the river.

Your first glance of this great gash in the earth may suggest that cataclysmic violence occurred here in remote geologic time. It wasn't quite that exciting. Erosion slowly did it, with scouring by the seasonally flood-swollen river, the rush of mud-laden side streams after heavy rains, occasional rock falls from high cliffs, and the relentless creep of landslides.

Actually the river established its course on soft, volcanic rocks. As the area gradually rose, the stream with its course committed, had no choice but to cut down through the older and harder basement rocks of Precambrian age, such as dark, platy schist, coarsely banded gneiss, and crystalline textured granite. Erosion is considerably slowed now by the upriver dam which separates the Monument from Curecanti National Recreation Area.

Elevation above sea level is about 2440 m (8000 feet) along both canyon rims. The climate is semi arid intermontane, with many microclimates between rim and canyon bottom. Precipitation, mostly in April and August, is about 46 cm (18 inches) a year. Temperature ranges from 29 C (mid 80's) in July and August to −27C (16°) below zero in winter.

For scenic beauty, this area would be hard to beat. Both north and south rims provide outstanding views, and there is a wealth of native plant and animal life.

Most conspicuous large mammal is the mule deer. Rarely a black bear or mountain lion is seen, and coyotes and bobcats are fairly common. Bird watching is popular, with several well defined habitats in which to look for particular species. Rock climbing and inner canyon trips may be done only under permit.

There are campgrounds on each rim. You should bring charcoal and water with you, although limited wood and water is furnished. For back country camping you must obtain a permit at park headquarters on the South Rim Drive. No overnight lodgings are available in the area, although light lunches, sandwiches and souvenirs are sold during summer at Rim House (South Rim).

The South Rim is open all year to Gunnison Point, by hard surface road from Montrose. The north rim, a 23 km (14 mile) graded road from Crawford and Delta is closed in winter. For information write the superintendent, at P.O. Box 1648, Montrose, Colorado 81401.

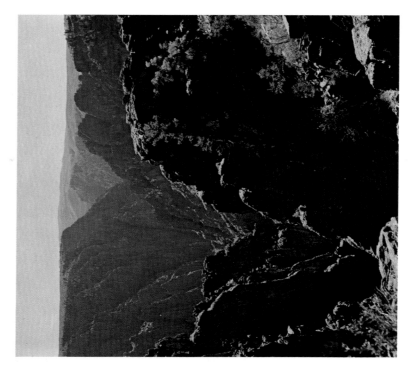

Bryce Canyon
UTAH

Within the Park you can travel along the jagged rim of the Paunsaugunt Plateau for 32 km (20 miles), looking over the famous Pink Cliffs of Bryce Canyon at the numberless weather-sculptured forms below the Rim. Here are the rainbow tints in stone which color a fantastic array of miniature cities, cathedrals, spires, windowed walls, and endless chessmen, shaped by forces of rain, frost, and running water working alternately through softer and harder limestone. From nearly any point along the southeast rim you look down into what appear to be communities provided with houses, schools, churches, theatres, all fashioned in stone and with inhabitants of various sizes, shapes and characteristics.

Park elevations range from a low of 2013 m (6,600 feet) on the edge of the Paria River valley to 2777 m (9,105 feet) at Rainbow Point near the south end of the Plateau. From the rim, averaging about 2440 m (8,000 feet), you can see, on a clear day, the massive dome of Navajo Mountain, 129 km (80 miles) away.

Your introduction to the Park should be at the visitor center. Here, displays unfold the story of this strange land and enable you to see "behind the vision" as you view the scenery later in a dozen indentations along the plateau rim. Park naturalists help you plan your visit within the time you have allotted, and with reference to the interpretive programs which begin in mid-May and end in late September.

You may wish to take any of a series of guided walks. Afterward, you are better prepared for the extensive marked trails; or you can cruise by auto along the 32 km (20 miles) of Rim road to the various amphitheaters and incredible views; or take the morning and afternoon horseback trips from the corral below the lodge, leading into the canyons and the very heart of the area.

Every evening during the summer, park ranger-naturalists give illustrated talks at the lodge and campfire circles on a different topic each night, from history to geology, to flowers and animals. There is much to learn of native life forms in the wide altitudinal and rainfall range here.

The Park road is open in winter to Sunset Point, Inspiration Point, Bryce Point, and Paria View, where many of the most famous formations may be seen. You may also enjoy winter activities such as snow shoeing, cross-country skiing, and snowmobiling. Concession operations are open from mid-May to early October. The lodge, near the rim of Bryce amphitheatre houses a lobby, dining room, gift shop, and soda fountain. Lodge accommodations are in cabins of two types, deluxe and standard. There is a laundry and shower facilities and store, near the North Campground. The store sells film, some groceries, and souvenirs. Cabin reservations are obtained by writing to: Utah Parks Division, TWA Services, Inc., Cedar City, Utah 84720.

The campgrounds, both administered by the National Park Service, are available from about May 15 to November 1, unless snow closes them earlier. Spaces are available not over 14 days per calendar year, per family. Facilities for tents and trailers, near water and restrooms, are equipped with tables and fireplaces. No reservations are made, so you must arrive early to get the most desired locations.

For information contact: The Superintendent, Bryce Canyon National Park, Bryce Canyon, Utah 84717.

Canyon de Chelly
ARIZONA

Completely surrounded by Indian Reservation, and actually a part of it, Canyon de Chelly (shay) is still lived in and farmed by the Navajos. This once remote area is now reached by all-weather paved roads from north and south. On the adjacent reservation, the Navajo Tribal Parks have installed rest stops for travelers, with shade, tables, fireplaces, and trash barrels at Wheatfields and Tsaile Lake.

Canyon de Chelly and its chief tributary, Canyon del Muerto, have cut channels through reddish sandstone to depths of 305 m (1,000 feet) in some places. Hundreds of natural caves in these cliffs provided shelter and dwellings sites for prehistoric Pueblo Indian farmers for centuries, until about A.D. 1300. Altitude range from canyon bottoms to mesa tops gave wide variety in plant and animal life, home and farm sites, and materials, all in a relatively small space. Moisture run-off from storms concentrated in sandy bottoms, to be conserved in restricted drainages instead of fanning out over wide-open areas to evaporate. Advantages in these vertical canyons, greater than in flat neighboring country, drew Navajos here about A.D. 1700.

The Navajos today, many of whom live in circular hogans (HO'ganz) of logs and poles, subsist mainly on wages, and partly on small-scale farming and their flocks. Their artistic handwoven rugs and silver work have become famous.

At the National Park Service headquarters and visitor center, elevation about 1676 m (5,500 feet) you can get information and best learn how to enjoy your visit. Because of quicksand, deep dry sand, and flash floods; to protect the many fragile ruins; and in respect for privacy of the Navajos, whose land it is — for these reasons, you are permitted to go into the canyons only if accompanied by a park ranger or an authorized guide. The only exception is that visitors may hike down to White House Ruin on the self-guiding trail from the canyon rim, a round trip hike of about 3.2 km (2 miles).

The 34 km (21-mile) paved road along the south rim of Canyon de Chelly provides access to the head of White House Trail, and to five scenic overlooks. At the end is Spider Rock Overlook, with fireplaces and "Chic Sales" restrooms. The 39 km (24-mile) paved road along the north rim of Canyon del Muerto provides access to four scenic overlooks.

If you wish to drive your own four-wheel drive vehicle into the canyons, you must arrange at the visitor center for a permit and an authorized guide. When conditions permit, the concessioner, the Thunderbird Lodge, offers commercial trips along the canyon floors in specially equipped vehicles. Horses with a Navajo guide are usually available or can be arranged for hire during the summer months.

The Thunderbird Lodge, dining room, and Indian art shop are officially open from April 1 through November 1. Reservations are advisable. The mail address is Chinle, Arizona 86503.

While camping in the canyons is not permitted, the National Park Service maintains excellent camping facilities at Cottonwood Campground, near Monument Headquarters. There are house trailer sites, but no trailer hookups. The campground is opened during the winter months. In it are restrooms, tables, and fireplaces. You should bring your own fuel. At nearby trading posts you can buy gasoline, groceries, and general merchandise daily. The superintendent's mailing address is Box 588, Chinle, Arizona 86503.

Canyonlands

UTAH

Canyonlands National Park, established in 1964, embraces over 1365 sq km (525 square miles) of superlative scenery in southwestern Utah. Minimal developments in roads, trails and campgrounds, consistent with preservation of wilderness values, have been, and are being, installed for visitor access and enjoyment.

Road approaches are from the north and east. Regular passenger cars can travel the graded dirt roads in much of the northern portion of the park, entering through The Neck and going across to the Island in the Sky. From here roads serve Grandview Point, Green River Overlook, and other points. Upheaval Dome, a very unusual feature of interest, is accessible by trail, and is only a short walk from the road.

From the east you enter the Needles district by a paved road extending 14 km (9 miles) into the Park, almost to Big Spring Canyon. The back country remains accessible only by foot and 4-wheel drive vehicles from the south or west. This is a rugged, isolated area, requiring overnight camping for even a short visit.

Squaw Flat Campground (27 sites) has the usual facilities, except for water, available about .8 km (½ mile) away. Otherwise, you should expect no water and be sure to carry it with you.

Beyond the auto roads are many miles of "jeep" road, often poorly marked. You should enter such roads only with 4-wheel drive, and after conferring with a park ranger. He will tell you how to avoid making new scars on the land, and how to enjoy a safe trip.

Pioneering efforts are being made at Canyonlands to devise new methods of preserving primitive values. You may find the occasional trash barrel an intrusion, but infinitely preferable to burying trash and having weather and wild creatures soon uncover it and scatter paper and cans!

Guided trips by jeep, horseback, and hiking, can be arranged; and for the real Canyonlands enthusiasts a float trip through Cataract Canyon is the ultimate experience. Ask a ranger for information, and be sure to use the registration system at ranger stations, to leave word of your destination and expected return time, in case of emergency. This method avoids needless rescue searches.

Elevations in the park range from about 1128 m (3,700 feet) in Cataract Canyon to nearly 2135 m (7,000 feet) at Cedar Mesa, with most of the land averaging 1525 m (5,000 feet) on the benches and 1830 m (6,000 feet) on the rims. The average annual precipitation is 12.5 to 22.5 cm (5 to 9 inches), occurring mostly in late-summer thunderstorms and winter snowfall on the rims. Normal high temperature is 37.8C to 40.4C (100 to 105 degrees) at most points, with winter seldom falling under −12C to −9C (10 to 15 degrees).

There are no overnight accommodations, eating places, gas stations, and very little water. The nearest public lodgings are in Monticello, to the southeast, and Moab, to the northeast. Both towns have camping supplies available.

Inquiries for additional information may be addressed to the park superintendent, 446 South Main, Moab, Utah 84532.

Capitol Reef

UTAH

This great buttressed sandstone cliff extends across 112 km (70 miles) of a vast wonderland of south central Utah. Wind and water have carved the escarpment into fantastic pinnacles, towers, and domes. In 1937, 1498 ha (3700 acres) were set aside as a National Monument, but in 1971 the status changed to a park and the acreage enlarged to 97,877 ha (241,671 acres). Along the route through the park you will see highly colored, grotesquely eroded cliffs, with colors strongest in the early morning or late afternoon.

You enter the 980 sq km (377 square mile) area on Utah 24, an excellent all-weather highway. Roads are open all year, except for occasional short periods after rain or snow. In addition there are 30 km (19 miles) of trails, on any of which you quickly get the feeling of remoteness.

The peculiar geographic isolation of the region made the Fremont River drainage the last section of Utah to be explored and settled by white man, although Indians for centuries had farmed the area along the river, fished in it, and hunted for game in the nearby mountains. Long ago they marked smooth cliff walls with petroglyphs of unusual style and size.

Vegetation, mammals and birds of Capitol Reef are typical of the Colorado Plateau's pinyon-juniper belt. Sagebrush, saltbrush and squawbush form much of the shrubby ground cover. Deer, foxes, bobcats, porcupines, and smaller rodents make up most of the mammal population. Lizards are abundant, but snakes are rarely seen. Hawks, owls, ravens and many other birds are common.

At the campground, about 1647 m (5,400 feet) elevation, the National Park Service has installed tables, fireplaces, running water and restrooms, and there is a small picnic area. Campers find daytime temperatures range from 27C to 32C (80 to 90 degrees), with normally cool nights. Spring and autumn are generally mild, but late December and January are cold.

The visitor center has exhibits on geology, archeology, and an illustrated orientation program. Special areas of interest near Utah 24 would include Hickman Bridge self-guiding nature trail and a 19 km (12 mile) scenic drive into Capitol Gorge. The more adventuresome visitor on trips into the North and South Districts of the park will see such attractions as Muley Twist Canyon, Halls Creek, Brimhall Natural Bridge, Cathedral Valley and South Desert. Hiking into more remote areas of the park should not be attempted without information from the Headquarters Office. For advance information about the park, write to the superintendent, Capitol Reef National Park, Torrey, Utah 84775.

13

Capulin Mountain

NEW MEXICO

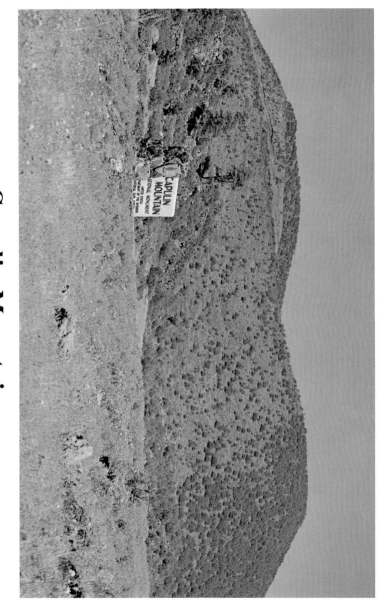

Capulin Mountain National Monument, established in 1916, contains 775 acres (314 ha) in the beautiful high plains country of northeastern New Mexico. The dominant feature is Capulin Mountain, a remarkably symmetrical cinder cone rising over 305 m (1,000 feet) above its base to an altitude of 2,494 m (8,182). The cone is approximately 6.4 km (4 miles) around the base, and the crater about 125 m (415 feet) deep.

Capulin Mountain is a conspicuous landmark, undoubtedly noticed by early pioneers on the Cimarron Cutoff of the famed Santa Fe Trail. A military freight cutoff trail passed near the mountain in the late 1880s. On clear days the visitor standing on the rim may see parts of New Mexico, Texas, Oklahoma, and Colorado, and to the west are the majestic, snow-capped peaks of the Sangre de Cristo Mountains.

Jutting out from the west base of this steep mountain — still so steep that rock fragments roll down it — is a rough and ragged jumble of rocks where a river of molten lava cooled and solidified. Above rise the ash-and-cinder slopes, tranquil now but once the scene of violent volcanic eruptions. Most of the cone today is lush with greenery of trees, shrubs, and grasses.

Recent studies indicate Capulin Mountain was active about 10,000 years ago, in the last stage of a great period of volcanic activity which was widespread throughout western North and South America. Typical of the older and more intense activity is Sierra Grande, an extinct volcano rising 670 m (2,200 feet) above the level plain about 16 km (10 miles) southeast. Northeast of Capulin a number of mesas are capped with black lavas from ancient flows. Some protective lava caps

have made older formations last longer than more recent ones.

Capulin's beauty lies partly in its abundant vegetation of mixed grassland and forest. Capulin is Spanish for chokecherry, and in addition to this shrub, pinyon, ponderosa pine, juniper, mountain mahogany, Gambel oak, skunkbush, and other larger plants are numerous. Early summer produces a wealth of wild flowers, including bluebells, daisies, Indian paintbrush, and lupines.

Mule deer, chipmunks, and ground squirrels are abundant and often seen. Over 100 species of birds have been seen here.

Perhaps the greatest enjoyment at Capulin is experienced on the mile-long (1.6 km) Crater Rim Trail, using the self-guiding booklet. It begins and ends at the parking area and has only a moderate climb. Another trail, leading from the parking area to the crater's bottom, enables you to see a volcanic mountain from the inside out.

The Monument is open year round, although the summit road is occasionally closed for a few days by heavy winter snows. Upon arrival you should stop at the visitor center, where you may see the exciting audio-visual film and obtain information from the park personnel on duty.

At the western base of the mountain is a picnic area, with water and modern restrooms. Camping is not permitted in the Monument; however a private campground is located in the village of Capulin.

A superintendent whose address is Capulin, New Mexico 88414, is in immediate charge of the Monument.

Carlsbad Caverns
NEW MEXICO

The dissolving action of underground water on limestone during the last one to five million years has produced these great caverns in extreme southeastern New Mexico. The entire fascinating geological story, from an organic reef around an ancient Permian sea (250 million years ago), covering by later sediments, upraising by crustal movements, saturation by percolating ground waters, and lowering of water table to create final form, is portrayed by exhibits in the Park's visitor center.

Development in many miles of subterranean passages and chambers has been restricted to the largest and most easily accessible parts of the 229 m (750 foot), and 253 m (829 foot) levels, which you reach by trail or elevator. The Big Room, 229 m (750 feet) below the surface and 1,113 m (3,650 feet) above sea level, has a 5.7 ha (14 acre) floor space, and is up to 78 m (225 feet) high.

Cavern trips are offered continuously from 8:00 a.m. to 3:15 p.m. in winter; from 7:00 a.m. to 6:00 p.m. in summer. Visitors may walk in through the natural entrance for a complete 4.8 km (3 mile) tour, or descend by elevator to take a 2 km (1¼ mile) walk around the Big Room. Visitors are each given a radio receiver that provides interpretive messages as they walk through the cave. Rangers are also available to answer questions, present interpretive talks and give visitors assistance throughout the cavern. Cavern temperature is about 13° C (56° F), so warm clothing is recommended, even though surface temperature may exceed 38° C (100° F). Comfortable walking shoes, with rubber soles or heels, are advisable. Return to the surface is by elevator.

Variety and size of stalactites and stalagmites in the vast chambers has made them renowned the world over. When wet, they gleam and appear translucent; dry, they appear dull and powdery.

Primitive hunting and gathering Indians roamed the region thousands of years ago. The fierce Apaches were encountered by Spanish explorers as they ventured northward along the nearby Pecos River in the late 1500's. Not until the 1880's did ranchers get into the mountainous country near the caverns. Jim White, a local cowboy and guano miner, began extensive exploration of the cave in 1901. The Park was created a national monument in 1923, becoming a national park by congressional action in 1930, and now embraces 190 sq km (73 sq miles).

The famous bat flights occur most evenings from April through October at the Cavern entrance, where a park naturalist explains the flight and discusses bats.

The surrounding Chihuahuan desert abounds with wildlife, including mule deer, pronghorns, jackrabbits, cottontails, squirrels, skunks, raccoons, foxes, and ringtails, and there is a long list of resident bird species. Desert reptiles are common. Desert plants are abundant, and many species are identified along paved trails in the park.

Guided lantern trips through undeveloped New Cave are available daily in summer and on weekends the rest of the year. Reservations are required for this strenuous trip. New Cave is an undeveloped cave located near the mouth of Slaughter Canyon 37 km (23 miles) from the park visitor center.

There are no overnight accommodations in the Park, but there are modern motels, and campgrounds in Carlsbad and White's City. Adjoining the visitor center in the Park are restaurant, curio shop, nursery, and kennel facilities. These services and the underground lunchroom are operated by Cavern Supply Company, Carlsbad, New Mexico, under government supervision, with rates approved by the National Park Service.

The park is administered by a superintendent, whose address is 3225 National Parks Highway, Carlsbad, New Mexico 88220.

Casa Grande Ruins

ARIZONA

The Casa Grande Ruins represent a unique example of foreign influences on prehistoric people in southern Arizona. New ideas in Mexico began to spread north about 300 B.C. By that time a new way of life had been introduced, possibly by immigration, which resulted in the development of the distinctive Hohokam culture of southern Arizona. The Hohokam in turn transmitted some of these new ideas farther to the north, planting the seed for the development of sedentary cultures elsewhere in the Southwest.

Mexican advances in architectural techniques and structures, crafts, and crops continued to influence the Hohokam for another 1600 years. During this period, these people lived in mud and wood houses, built ceremonial courts, and extended an irrigation canal system on the higher terraces of the Gila and Salt Valleys, to an eventual total length of about 805 km (500 miles).

In the 1200's and 1300's a new wave of outside influences spread through the Hohokam area. Large Mexican-type caliche-walled contiguous dwellings were built at this time. Many villages were planned and constructed as rectangular walled compounds. A colorful style of pottery made by Pueblo Indians to the northeast was imported in great quantities. Indeed, some of the people themselves may have moved in and settled among the Hohokam.

The "Big House" at Casa Grande, dated near A.D. 1300, may have reflected a new ceremonial concept derived from Mexico. While the exact purpose of the Big House is not known, there are indications that it may have been used at times as an astronomical observatory.

Meanwhile, environmental forces were working against the Hohokam. Long irrigation had waterlogged much of the best farming land, causing salt and other alkaline substances to rise and re-deposit near the surface, gravely limiting crop development. Major climatic changes may have added to their problems.

In 1694, when the Jesuit missionary priest Father Eusebio Kino first visited Casa Grande, this large site, as well as all others in the region, was in ruin. Nearby Pima Indians, the probable descendants of the prehistoric Hohokam-Pueblo development, living in small wood and mud houses but lacking heavy-walled structures, were irrigating a large acreage on the flood plains along the river.

In 1891, the Smithsonian Institution undertook the first excavations at Casa Grande, and in the following year the ruins were set aside as a reserve. In 1918 it was designated a National Monument. Located at Coolidge, Arizona, the 191 ha (472 acre) area is accessible by paved highway. Exhibits portray the life of the ancient people, and guide service is offered several times daily. Self-guiding walking tours can be taken near, but not into, the Big House.

Hot summer and warm winter days are common in the Lower Sonoran Desert elevation of 434 m (1,422 feet). Complete tourist accommodations are available in nearby towns. There are no camping facilities, but limited picnic space is available near headquarters. The annual permit is valid here. The address of the superintendent in charge is, P.O. Box 518, Coolidge, Arizona 85228.

16

Cedar Breaks

UTAH

In the Markagunt Plateau of southwestern Utah, a rugged limestone slope has weathered into a gigantic, multicolored amphitheater, with altitudes from 2552 m (8,100 feet) to 3263 m (10,700 feet). The "breaks" occur where the plateau rim breaks into high cliffs and steep talus slopes. The so-called "cedars" are really junipers, growing at elevations well below the rim. Approach roads are through heavy forests of pine, fir, spruce, and aspen; the rim is dotted with subalpine meadows and thickets of Engelmann spruce and subalpine fir. Of special interest are the bristlecone pines, with one over 1,600 years old. This tree grows to timberline here, at about 3416 m (11,200 feet).

Moist and fertile soil provides lavish July and August flower displays, including fringed gentians, columbines, penstemons, bluebells, and Indian paintbrush. Wildlife includes Clark's nutcracker and the violet-green swallow and white-throated swift. Mule deer are the only large mammals. Marmots den among the rocks; weasels, badgers, picas, and porcupines are common; and ground squirrels, chipmunks, and red squirrels scurry about gathering spruce cones for winter food.

Exploration of the Plateau started with Mormon settlements at Parowan and Cedar City in 1851. Later came the Wheeler-Powell Surveys, followed by many years of timber and grazing use. First protection was given in 1905 under the U.S. Forest Service, and since 1933 the 25 sq km (9½ square mile) area has been a National Monument under care of the National Park Service.

The road into Cedar Breaks is not kept open year round. The road is plowed clear of snow in April or May and may be closed again in October or November.

To obtain maximum enjoyment, start at the visitor center, a mile from the south entrance, where you can see the natural history exhibits and receive suggestions and information. Take the 8 km (5 mile) Rim Drive from Point Supreme to North View, with side roads and paths to viewpoints. The Wasatch Ramparts Trail runs from Point Supreme for 3.2 km (2 scenic miles) to the bristlecone pines. A short trail leads to Alpine Pond. At nearby Brian Head, in the National Forest, is a superb view from 3,451 m (11,315 feet).

Near Point Supreme is the picnic and campground area. Trailers are welcome, but there are no utility connections. The non-freezing summer weather allows comfortable camping from late June to early September.

The nearest lodging and meals are located at Brian Head Ski Resort or at Cedar City.

For general information about the monument, write to the superintendent, Cedar Breaks National Monument, Box 749, Cedar City, Utah 84720.

Chaco Canyon
NEW MEXICO

One of the world's largest prehistoric apartment houses was the 4-story, 800 room Pueblo Bonito. It is in Chaco Canyon, northwestern New Mexico, with a dozen other large pueblos and a great many smaller prehistoric sites of the Anasazi, as well as historic sites of the later Navajos. Since 1907 this region has been protected as part of the 87 sq km (33½ sq mi) Chaco Canyon National Monument, administered by the National Park Service.

Human history began here about 10,000 years ago with arrival of wandering big game hunters. After big game disappeared they hunted smaller animals and gathered native plants. In about A.D. 1 the Basketmakers made their homes here, lived in pit houses, made fine baskets, and raised corn, beans and squash. By A.D. 700 (approx) they had refined all their technological skills and begun building stone houses. These changes marked beginning of the later Anasazi or Pueblo Indians.

The Chacoans reached a cultural peak in the mid 1000's, living in huge urban pueblos such as Pueblo Bonito and building sophisticated roadways, stairways and irrigation systems. Many great kivas, communal ceremonial chambers in which large groups gathered, were built. Pottery and jewelry making and other crafts flourished, and some of the Southwest's finest architecture developed here then.

Reasons for this "blossoming" of Chaco culture are not exactly known. Some evidence suggests an extensive trade system provided contacts with other people as far south as Mexico and north to Mesa Verde, stimulating the economy and advancing the technology.

Population increased rapidly as immigrants came from neighboring areas, until at its peak there were probably 5,000 people here. Then the Chacoans began leaving their canyon homes in the mid 12th century. Reasons for abandonment aren't clear — possibly problems of soil depletion, poor sanitation, disease, economic collapse, internal bickering, or combinations of these problems brought the exodus which was completed in the late 1200's.

The Monument is open year round. Daytime temperatures may reach the high 90's in summer, and on cold winter nights get well below freezing. This high, semi-arid plateau region of 1,922 m (6,300 feet) elevation has frequent but scattered thunder showers from July through September, and sometimes several inches of winter snow. Juniper and pinyon growth covers the higher mesas, with saltbush and black greasewood common on the canyon floor.

Gasoline, food, lodging and repair services are not available at the Monument, although a limited assortment of staple foods and gasoline is usually obtainable on week days at nearby trading posts.

A mile from the visitor center is a 35 unit campground, with tables, fireplaces, water, restrooms, and turnouts for small trailers, but no utility connections. You should bring your own fuel. In winter the campground has no water, and pit toilets only. Camping fees: $2.00 in summer; no fees October 15–April 15.

Stop first at the visitor center, where museum exhibits help you understand the area and its prehistory. Many of the major ruins are near the road paralleling the north side of the canyon, and are easy to reach over short trails.

Hour-long self-guiding ruins trails reach Casa Rinconada, Chettro Kettle, Pueblo del Arroyo and Pueblo Bonito. For information about conducted tours and special evening programs, ask at the visitor center. Representatives of large groups should write or phone in advance for special services or assistance with group camping. Mail address of the resident superintendent is Star Route #4, Box 6500, Bloomfield, New Mexico 87413. Telephone 505 — 786-5384.

Chamizal National Memorial

TEXAS

Chamizal National Memorial, dedicated in 1973, is located on 22 ha (54.9 acres) of land acquired from the Republic of Mexico in the Chamizal Settlement of 1963. The Memorial commemorates the history of the boundary between the two nations, from 1848 to the present.

Through a documentary film and a small permanent museum the story of the initial boundary surveys, 1849–57, presents one of the most dramatic physical and human adventures of Western North America, against a backdrop of 3200 km (2000 miles) of unsurveyed and difficult terrain. Equally important, the human adventure of the surveys and the resolution of land and water problems presents a demonstration of the far-reaching results of men working together towards equitable solutions of vexing problems — and gaining friendship and understanding as a result of their common efforts.

To keep the spirit of Chamizal alive, the auditorium, which during the day presents an exceptional documentary film, becomes a live theater at night, presenting internationally known artists at very reasonable prices. Annually, on the first weekend of October, the Border Folk Festival brings together the many varieties of music, dances, and crafts from the border states of Mexico and the United States, including performances by Indian groups.

Chamizal National Memorial is located immediately west of the Cordova Island Port of Entry and is accessible from either Paisano Drive or Delta Drive. Among the interesting aspects of a visit is the Chamizal Park of Mexico, across the international boundary. In Mexico, attractions include 308 ha (760 acres) of landscaped area related to the Chamizal Settlement of 1963, museum, crafts center, and excellent restaurants. Enroute, be sure to notice the statue of Abraham Lincoln, on Avenida Lincoln. The statue is dedicated to the spirit of international friendship expressed by Lincoln.

The Memorial is administered by a superintendent, whose address is 620 Southwest National Bank Building, 300 East Main Drive, El Paso, Texas 79901, telephone (915) 543-7780.

Chickasaw National Recreation Area

OKLAHOMA

Here the eastern hardwood forest meets the western plains. In places the transition from woods to surrounding prairie is so abrupt that it is possible to sit in the shade of the woods while admiring the blooms of prairie plants and even such desert plants as cactus and yucca.

At the north edge of the ancient Arbuckle Mountains, spring fed streams flow through forested valleys. Cool springs, clear streams with calm pools interspersed with riffles and small waterfalls, rocky bluffs, grassy hillsides, and quiet forest groves provide a tranquil place for recreation, so welcome in our fast paced urban world. Lake of the Arbuckles, a 952 ha (2,350 acre) man made lake in the southwestern part of the Recreation Area, is a place for more energetic water activities, fishing, boating, swimming, and water skiing.

The presence of mineral springs, in a time when they were generally believed to have medicinal properties, led to establishment of Sulphur Springs Reservation in 1902, in the Chickasaw Nation, Indian Territory. The area was renamed Platt National Park in 1906 to commemorate Orville Hitchcock Platt, late Senator from Connecticut. The National Park Service assumed responsibility for the recreational use of nearby Arbuckle Recreation Area in 1965. Platt National Park and Arbuckle Recreation Area were joined in 1976, and renamed Chickasaw National Recreation Area in recognition of the Chickasaw Indian Nation to which the land once belonged.

Your first stop should be at Travertine Nature Center, where exhibits and other interpretive activities will help you make the most of your visit. You can get a comprehensive scenic view of the oldest part of the Recreation Area by taking the 9.6 km (6 mile) perimeter drive. About 24 km (15 miles) of trails provide access to points of interest. With both prairie and forest, more than 600 species of plants grow in the area. The diversity of habitat provides a place for many kinds of birds and animals. Cardinals and eastern fox squirrels are always about, roadrunners, armadillos and rabbits are occasionally seen. Beaver, bobcat, deer, fox, opossum, raccoon and skunk are also common but seldom seen. There is a small herd of bison.

Travertine Nature Center is open daily with a park naturalist on duty to answer questions or help plan visits. In summer daily guided walks and other programs and activities help you learn more about the area and the place of humans in the natural world. Similar programs may be scheduled for groups at other seasons, if requested at least two weeks in advance.

There are extensive picnic and camping facilities. Advance reservations may be made for campsites in the summer season. Camping is limited to 14 days in summer, 30 days the rest of the year.

For further information write the Superintendent, Chickasaw National Recreation Area, P.O. Box 201, Sulphur, Oklahoma 73086.

Chiricahua

ARIZONA

The Chiricahua Mountains have been described as a "mountain island in a sea of grass." Tucked in the southeastern corner of Arizona, 58 km (36 miles) from Willcox, and 113 km (70 miles) from Douglas, the first time visitor is amazed to find this forested area which presents a variety of trees, shrubs, and wildflowers for his enjoyment.

Perhaps the dominant feature of the Monument is the assortment of fantastic rock formations shaped by nature into slender pinnacles, balanced rocks, and weird likenesses of giant animals and men. The early settlers called the area "Wonderland of Rocks" because of these unique volcanic sculptures carved by erosion in the rhyolite lavas.

Millions of years ago, nearby volcanoes spewed forth white-hot ash which welded into rock, later to be split by block faulting and tension and compression fractures so that weathering could widen and deepen the openings. A combination of adequate rainfall, about 45 cm (18 inches) in modern times, and rich soil produces a wealth of plant types ranging from cactus and desert grassland types at the lowest elevation of 1574 m (5160 feet) to the junipers, pines, and even occasional Douglas-firs at the highest elevation of 2246 m (7,365 feet).

Within this 44 sq km (17 square mile) Monument, created in 1924, the visitor can see abundant wildlife, including white-tail deer, coati-mundis, javelinas, bobcats, porcupines, coyotes, foxes, skunks, and the rare Apache fox squirrel. Reptiles are common, but only the rattlesnakes and rarely seen coral snakes are dangerous. The Monument is a paradise for bird observers, especially for its concentration of flycatcher species, and in springtime for the warbler migrations.

In an area rich in natural history, man has also had an impact. These mountains were a fortress for the Chiricahua Apaches. Under their famous leader, Cochise, they made life precarious for travelers on the Butterfield Stage line, a few miles to the north at Apache Pass. An historic peace treaty was achieved in 1886. White men began to settle in this district in the 1880's and brought cattle into lower Bonita Canyon.

Arriving visitors should stop at the Monument headquarters, one mile inside the boundary, where they pay the admission fee of $1.00 per carload, or show their annual pass. At the visitor center they may see exhibits about the area and be advised of any activities or services available. Afterward, visitors should take the 9.6 km (6 mile) scenic road to Massai Point parking area, where they will see superlative scenery and be able to visit a small geology exhibit.

More than 26 km (16 miles) of trails lead to points of interest, with hikes of from 20 minutes to 5½ hours. Wear comfortable shoes and carry water on longer trips.

The campground, elevation 1629 m (5,340 feet) is open year round, and has water, picnic tables, fire grates, and restrooms. Firewood gathering is not permitted, so visitors should bring their own wood or charcoal. Several sites can accommodate trailers up to 6 m (20 feet) long, but lack utility hookups. A $2.00/night/vehicle camping fee is charged. Summer camping is limited to 14 days. Temperatures are generally mild, but weather can be very cold and unpredictable in winter.

Mail address of the resident superintendent is Dos Cabezas Star Route, Willcox, Arizona 85643.

Colorado National Monument

COLORADO

Colorado National Monument preserves and protects a portion of that giant and ruggedly beautiful land between Colorado's central western border and the meeting place of the powerful Colorado and Gunnison rivers. Established in 1911, the monument's 73 sq km (28 square miles) embraces part of the great upwarp in the earth's crust known as the Uncompahgre Highland, where erosive forces have carved out vividly colored cliffs and monoliths towering 460 m (1500 feet) above the green carpeted Grand Valley of the Colorado.

Numerous steep-walled canyons and sparsely distributed springs determine the arid-land habitat and environment of many plant and animal types. Average annual rainfall is about 28 cm (11 inches). Typical altitudes range between 1426 m (4674 feet) at the downstream entrance to 1543 m (5058 feet) at the east entrance, to 2025 m (6640 feet) on Rim Rock Drive.

The area is like a geology text book in full color, plus being tri-dimensional. There are Precambrian rocks here over a billion years old; then, just east of the monument on Grand Mesa are lavas less than a million years old. The core of the Uncompahgre was ancient granite, gneiss, schist, and pegmatite dikes. During hundreds of millions of years, this highland eroded away, covered alternately with stream and lake deposits and dunes of wind-blown sand. Then, about the time the Rocky Mountains were being formed, tremendous earth forces lifted the Uncompahgre Plateau above the surrounding country.

Mountain-making uplifts cracked the earth's crust into a 16 km (10 mile) long fault, which today forms a conspicuous escarpment hundreds of feet high, crossing the monument. Add the never ending forces of erosion by rain, frost action and wind, and we have the corridor-like canyons, towering monoliths, and weird rock formations. Erosion has also uncovered petrified logs and dinosaur bones over 100 million years old.

Prehistoric basketmaker Indians once lived in the area, and more recently the Utes were here. The Spanish came very near in 1776, as recorded by Fray Escalante for a party en route from Santa Fe to Monterey, California. Many trappers visited Fort Robideaux, established south of the Monument in 1830.

The monument is easily reached by highway, and special sightseeing trips are scheduled in summer from Grand Junction, where cars may also be rented. Nature walks and evening programs are conducted in summer, with programs posted in public use areas. Exhibits in the visitor center explain prehistory, history, and natural history. Several self-guiding nature trails along canyon rims are enjoyable. For longer trail hikes carry water, and notify a ranger at headquarters of your hiking plans.

At the Saddlehorn, near the west entrance, is a campground and picnic area, with tables, fireplaces, water, firewood and restrooms. Near the east entrance is a picnic area, with shelter, restrooms, charcoal grills and tables. Food, motels, gas and camping supplies are not available in the monument, but may be had in nearby towns.

A superintendent, whose address is Colorado National Monument, Fruita, Colorado 81521, is in immediate charge.

Coronado
ARIZONA

Coronado National Memorial, a 1148 ha (2,834 acre) strip of grassland and rugged mountains, is located at the southeastern tip of the Huachuca Mountains adjoining the Mexican boundary in southeastern Arizona. The Memorial commemorates the first extensive European penetration into what was to become the United States. From Coronado Peak's commanding elevation of 2094 m (6,864 feet), one overlooks the San Pedro River Valley which served as the route for Coronado and his men.

In 1536, Cabeza de Vaca, Estevan the Black, and two companions, survivors of the ill-fated Narvaez expedition to Florida, arrived in Mexico City after eight years of wandering through the Southwest, Texas, and northern Mexico. They brought tales of a land to the north which contained great cities and fabulous riches in gold, silver, and precious stones. Mendoza, the Spanish Viceroy of Mexico, sent Fray Marcos de Niza and Estevan, a Negro slave, to investigate these reports in 1539. In leading the advance guard into the unknown land to the north, Estevan became the first non-Indian to enter this part of the Southwest. He apparently reached Cibola, where he was killed. When word reached Fray Marcos, who was following some distance behind, he called off further exploration and returned to Mexico with glowing stories of the legendary Seven Cities of Cibola.

Mendoza, now convinced, selected Francisco Vasquez de Coronado as the leader of a large expedition to claim Cibola for Spain. In February, 1540, an army of over 300 Spanish soldiers, 800 Indians, and four priests headed north from Compostela, Mexico. In June of the same year this army of explorers passed within sight of Coronado Peak as they entered what is now the United States. Cibola, the group of Zuni villages in western New Mexico, was reached in July, 1540. Instead of finding the cities of fabulous wealth, the Spaniards were met by hostile Indians in stone age towns.

Visitors to the Memorial headquarters near the mouth of Montezuma Canyon, 1626 m (5,330 feet) elevation, will find historical exhibits in the visitor center, and a place to relax in the nearby picnic ground. The area was established by presidential proclamation in 1952 to permanently commemorate the Spanish exploration as an important milestone in Southwestern history.

A winding graded road leads from the headquarters up to the Montezuma Pass parking area. From here the visitor can take a short self-guided nature trail to Coronado Peak and a magnificent view, where the eye can penetrate for more than 80 km (50 miles) into Mexico. Those interested in natural history and scenery may walk the 4.8 km (3 mile) Joe's Canyon Trail back to Headquarters via Smugglers Ridge and a wooded canyon. Several species of desert high altitude plants such as cactus, sotol, and agave, plus live oaks, pinyon pine, juniper, and lesser vegetation can be seen. Birds are abundant throughout the year, and some of the uncommon mammals of this area are the coati, Coues deer, and peccary.

There are no overnight camping facilities in the Memorial although there is a public campground in the nearby Coronado National Forest; the surrounding towns offer excellent tourist accommodations. A superintendent is in charge, and lives in the area. His mailing address is: Rural Route 1, Box 126, Hereford, Arizona 85615.

Curecanti
COLORADO

Centered high in Colorado's Rocky Mountains, Curecanti National Recreation Area attracts visitors the year round for boating, water-skiing and fishing in summer and ice fishing, cross-country skiing and snow-mobiling in winter. Named for Curicata, a Ute Indian chief who roamed and hunted over the Colorado Territory, the recreation area is composed of three lakes, Blue Mesa, Morrow Point and Crystal. These lakes are formed by dams built on the Gunnison River by the Bureau of Reclamation as part of the Upper Colorado River Storage Project authorized by Congress in 1956.

Blue Mesa Lake, the largest lake in Colorado when filled to capacity, provides the primary recreation facilities. Here the visitor can find campgrounds, a visitor center with scheduled interpretive activities in summer, free concrete boat launching ramps, and two marinas with rental boats for fishing and waterskiing, rental slips, fuel, fishing equipment, boat repair service, and camping supplies.

At different seasons of the year, Blue Mesa Lake offers some of the best lake fishing in Colorado. The Colorado Division of Wildlife in cooperation with the U.S. Fish and Wildlife Service maintains a fish stocking program planting several million fish each year. The most commonly caught fish is the rainbow trout, followed by the brown trout, Kokanee salmon and mackinaw trout.

In a land characterized by long, hard winters and short, beautiful summers, Blue Mesa Lake usually is entirely frozen over sometime early in January. Open water generally appears late in March with the lake becoming completely navigable in April.

Winter visitors have the opportunity to see wintering herds of deer and elk that number in the hundreds. Also in winter, golden and bald eagles are commonly seen, along with hundreds of water and shore birds in spring.

Much of the railroad bed of the historic Denver and Rio Grande narrow gauge line which ran between Salida and Montrose is now under water. However, one very important monument has been preserved. At Cimarron, 32 km (20 miles) east of Montrose, on one of the original narrow gauge trestles sits narrow gauge engine #278 with its tender loaded with coal, a freight car and a caboose. Restored to its condition of the late 1930's, the train exhibit stands in silent tribute to a never-to-be-forgotten era of railroading in the Colorado Rockies. Following a path that years earlier was considered impassable by Captain John Gunnison, a surveyor, the narrow gauge trains carrying coal, livestock, lumber, grain and other goods provided communication and transport in the early pioneer west.

At Cimarron also, self-guiding tours of the Bureau of Reclamation's 143 m (469 foot) high Morrow Point Dam and its automated, underground power plant are available in the summer months.

Free tour boat rides offered daily during the summer season afford magnificent views of the cliffs and spires of Morrow Point Lake, which stretches for eleven miles along the bottom of a deep, narrow fiord-like canyon. Additional information on boat tours and the recreation area is available from the superintendent, P.O. Box 1040, Gunnison, Colorado 81230.

Dinosaur National Monument

COLORADO — UTAH

Dinosaur National Monument, best known for its excellent assemblage of dinosaur fossils, is also the site of a rugged expanse of deeply incised canyons formed by the Green and Yampa Rivers. The monument, which straddles the states of Utah and Colorado, attracts a wide variety of people including boaters, horseback riders, scientists, and family vacationers.

The Dinosaur Quarry, discovered in 1909 by Earl Douglass of the Carnegie Museum, is the main visitor attraction. The Quarry site, which represents an ancient dinosaur "sandbar cemetery," contains a large concentration of fossils. Fourteen varieties of dinosaur, two crocodiles, and three turtles have been found, all from the Jurassic period of earth history, 140 million years ago. Although the fossils are no longer being removed, visitors can watch technicians uncover and relief the huge fossil bones on the cliff face. A unique, modern visitor center completely encloses the Quarry site and allows visitors to view the Quarry operations year around.

Although the majority of visitors arriving at Dinosaur know little about the canyon area of the monument, those who take the time to discover its many scenic features are well rewarded. For most visitors who see Dinosaur by car, the 50 km (31 mile) drive to Harpers Corner is the best way to view the canyons. The drive begins at Monument Headquarters 1.6 km (1 mile) east of the town of Dinosaur, Colorado, on U.S. Highway 40. Various scenic overlooks along the road with interpretive exhibits help the visitor understand the geology and natural history of the area. A 3 km (2 mile) hiking trail at Harpers Corner leads to the rim of the Green River canyon, where a 793 m (2,600 foot) drop to the bottom of the gorge provides a breathtaking view. Those with more time can take a 21 km (13 mile) dirt road down to Echo Park, the confluence of the Green and Yampa Rivers.

An increasing number of people each year are getting away from their cars and seeing the river canyons by rubber raft or kayak. River permits are required for all boating use of the rivers within the Monument. Those people without the experience or equipment to attempt a float trip themselves, can go with experienced guides from one of the concession operators. White water rapids on both the Yampa and Green Rivers provide excitement and challenge for even the most experienced boatmen. Glimpses of a Rocky Mountain Bighorn Sheep or a flock of Canada Geese are some of the potential rewards for taking the time to see Dinosaur by water.

Camping is best during the spring, summer, and early fall. Split Mountain and Green River Campgrounds, near the Quarry Visitor Center, are easily accessible from U.S. Highway 40. Primitive campgrounds at Echo Park, Deerlodge Park, and the Gates of Lodore are favorites with visitors wanting to enjoy the less traveled areas of the monument.

For more information write to the superintendent, Dinosaur National Monument, Dinosaur, Colorado 81610.

El Morro

NEW MEXICO

Imagine a newspaper weighing several million tons, in one perpetual edition, covering a time range of more than 800 years! Such is El Morro, the famous "Inscription Rock" of west-central New Mexico. Here, at 7,200 feet (2196 m) above sea level, a 200 foot (61 m) monolithic headland (morro in Spanish) of sandstone rises above a smooth valley floor to form a striking landmark visible for many miles. A large pool that collected rain and melted snow at the base of the cliff provided a considerable and dependable supply of water for anyone passing through this region.

Long before the Spanish came, ancestors of the Zuni Indians lived in 14th Century pueblos atop "The Rock," and made hundreds of inscriptions on smooth surfaces near the cliff base. After these people had moved away in the 1400's, Spaniards, 100 years later, carved records of their passage, and later yet, Americans.

The earliest known Spanish inscription was made in 1605 by Don Juan de Oñate, first provincial governor of New Mexico. Later inscriptions sometimes consisted only of names and dates. Others recorded exploring and missionary expeditions, and told of death and disaster and punitive journeys. Still others revealed personal characteristics of wit and ego.

The earliest inscription in English is dated 1849, when Lt. J. H. Simpson, U.S.A., and R. H. Kern, artist, copied the older carvings.

El Morro and the surrounding 1,278 acres (518 ha) were established as a national monument in 1906. There is an all-weather access road, and the area is open year-round. Heavy snows sometimes occur in winter, and temperatures drop quite low. The most delightful time for visiting, weatherwise, is from May through October. Summer days are warm; nights are crisp. But the winter view, when soft snow falls, is outstanding, and visitors prepared for the weather can enjoy a visit then. There is a picnic area, and a primitive, 9 site, campground. There are no camping fees.

Your first stop should be at the visitor center where you may learn of the region's history. From here you can follow a self-guiding trail, with numbered stations, wayside exhibits, and a guide leaflet. The hike past the inscriptions and back, requires 40 minutes. Or, you may extend the hike to an hour and a half by taking the scenic path over the mesa top and visiting the Indian ruins there. This is also a good area for taking photographs and observing birds. A visitor might be fortunate enough to see a golden eagle. In summer, swifts and swallows are numerous.

The mesa top, as is explained in the trail booklet, exhibits several interesting aspects relating to the geologic story of this ancient land.

The plant life is a blend of grassland and sage with the pinyon-juniper border of the ponderosa pine forest, represented here only by scattered clumps of the stately trees. Gambel oak thrives on the north side of El Morro, and four-winged salt-bush and rabbitbrush do quite well. Bee spiderflower, big snakeweed, groundsel, tansyleaf aster, four-o'clock, and spiderwort are characteristic.

The superintendent's address is: El Morro National Monument, Ramah, New Mexico 87321.

Florissant Fossil Beds

COLORADO

You approach this area through rolling hills and ridges covered with ponderosa pine, Douglas-fir, Colorado blue spruce and aspen. In season you also find this valley glorious with abundant wild flowers. Florissant was named in 1870 after Florissant, Missouri, a suburb of St. Louis, from which Judge James Castello came. Whether or not the many flowers which bloom here caused him to name the town as he did, is not positively known. Florissant is a French word meaning flowering or blooming.

Here, hidden several feet under the earth surface, are the famous fossil beds, believed the world's most extensive deposit of delicate, fossilized insects and leaves. There are superbly preserved impressions of 35 million year old dragon flies, butterflies, beetles, ants, spiders and fish. Leaves of birches, willows, maples, beeches, etc., as well as needles from fir and giant sequoias are abundant. Even palm leaves occur, testifying to a once warmer climate.

The fossils were created between 34–35 million years ago, during the Oligocene Epoch. A volcanic field near Guffy, about 27 km (17 miles) southwest of Florissant, erupted during this period. The volcanic ash, dust and pumice was wind-carried over ancient Lake Florissant and ultimately created shales in the lakebed.

Like pages of an album, these layers preserve an amazingly accurate record of plants and animals once living around the lake. The fossil area was discovered by Dr. A. C. Peale, U.S. Geological Survey, in 1874. Since then scientists from the world over have dug into the shale, removed many thousands of specimens, and identified over 1,100 insect and 144 plant species.

Among the discoveries were petrified tree stumps, including a Sequoia stump 3.4 m (11 feet) high, with diameter of 3 m (10 feet). When the trees were alive the area was about 915 m (3,000 feet) above sea level; now it is at 2,532 m (8,300 feet).

Ancient Lake Florissant was formed by a lava flow damming a stream, making a sickle-shaped lake 19 km (12 miles) long and up to 3.2 km (2 miles) wide. Later mud flows covered the shale beds and many lake shore trees. A final series of massive eruptions covered the area with lava and compressed the shale layers under lava crust which preserved the forming shales for millions of years.

Today the National Monument, created by Act of Congress August 20, 1969, embraces over 23 sq km (9 square miles) of Federal lands. Visitors enjoy lush grassland meadows. Squirrels, prairie dogs, coyotes, badgers, rabbits, porcupines, mule deer and elk are sometimes seen. Bluebirds, warblers, nuthatches, mountain chickadees, even golden eagles may be seen.

At the visitor center, 4 km (2-½ miles) south of the village of Florissant, a park ranger is at your service. Here examples of the fossils may be seen, and a nature trail and picnic area are adjacent. Overnight facilities are available in Pike National Forest and nearby towns.

A word of caution: Ticks, possibly disease bearing, are common in spring and early summer. Check yourself periodically for ticks and if any become imbedded consult a ranger or physician.

For information contact the superintendent, Florissant Fossil Beds National Monument, P.O. Box 185, Florissant, Colorado 80816.

Fort Bowie

ARIZONA

Authorized by Congress in August 1964, and formally dedicated as such in 1972, Fort Bowie National Historic Site contains 393 ha (970 acres) dedicated to preserving the Butterfield Overland Mail Route, the Apache Pass Stage Station, Apache Spring, and the Fort Bowie complex.

Ruins stabilization work has been done on Fort buildings periodically since 1967, and will continue. The purpose is not to restore but to preserve against the ravages of time and weather. Visitor facilities will be limited to portrayal, through exhibits and park interpreters, of the events and personalities which made history here. For this is an exciting story, compounded of action and heroism. A gallant band of Chiricahua Indians tried to stop the westward march of the equally gallant soldiers, who formed the vanguard of white man's westward expansion. Bitter fighting which focused here forced the Army to develop sophisticated guerrilla warfare techniques, with help of Apache scouts, thus making these long-ago events pertinent to today in the adage: ''The Past is Prologue to the Future.''

There is no road into the ruins of Fort Bowie. You reach them by the 2.4 km (1-½ mile) foot trail which begins toward the eastern section of Apache Pass. At the Fort area there is usually a park ranger on duty in a small ranger station-museum, to provide interpretation and enforce regulations. There are no camping or picnic facilities in the park. Nearest campground is at Chiricahua National Monument, 40 km (25 miles) away, and there are motels, stores and trailer parks in the nearby towns of Willcox and Bowie. Inquiries for information may be addressed to: Park Ranger in Charge, Fort Bowie National Historic Site, P.O. Box 158, Bowie, Arizona 85605.

28

Fort Davis

TEXAS

Fort Davis (1854–1891) best preserved of the Southwestern military posts under administration of the National Park Service, is the principal feature of Fort Davis National Historic Site, Texas. In 1963, 181 ha (447 acres) were set aside to preserve the remnants of more than 60 stone and adobe structures, and 5 ha (13 acres) were added later.

In 1849, the Army surveyed two major routes across West Texas, from San Antonio to the El Paso area. More than 60,000 travelers to California took this trail in the early 1850's. Near Fort Davis, this trail crossed one of the regular routes of the Southern Plains Indians, used for their forays into Mexico. To protect travelers, maintain communications, and deny nearby water sources to the Indians, Fort Davis was established on October 23, 1854. Apart from a period of abandonment during the Civil War, it was active for 37 years, and was among the most significant posts of the Mescalero Apache campaigns, 1869 through 1881. Of the twelve regiments which served at Fort Davis, the 8th Infantry, 9th and 10th Cavalry, and 24th and 25th Infantry were most prominent.

Apart from its strategic significance, the site was selected by the Army because of "salubrious" climate and excellent water supply. Nestled in a small canyon on the flanks of the Davis Mountains, at an elevation of 1495 m (4,900 feet), Fort Davis adds a touch of historic drama to the scenic splendor of the Davis Mountains, second highest range in Texas. Situated at the northern edge of the town of Fort Davis, the fort may be reached from several highway approaches. Nearest large communities are Alpine, 42 km (26 miles) to the southeast, and Marfa, 34 km (21 miles) to the southwest.

There are no campgrounds, but there are picnic facilities in the Historic Site. Davis Mountain State Park, which abuts the area on the north and west, provides lodge, restaurant, camping and picnicking sites. Motels in Fort Davis, Alpine, and Marfa provide restaurant motel, and shopping facilities, and both Alpine and Marfa have hotels.

Arriving visitors will enter the Site by way of the visitor center, placed inside a reconstructed Army barracks of the 1860's, and containing a museum, an audio-visual room and a complete range of visitor services. From there, self-guiding trails take them through the historic area. An especially pleasant walk is the climb up North Ridge, along a self-guiding nature trail which offers a splendid view of the fort. Of special interest, also, are the audio programs, which present period bugle calls at appropriate times of the day, and a re-enactment, in sound, of an 1875 Retreat Parade as it would have been heard at Fort Davis.

Inquiries may be mailed to the Superintendent, Box 1456, Fort Davis, Texas 79734.

Fort Larned

KANSAS

Fort Larned, in today's peaceful rural setting of southwest Kansas, is a reminder of a highly significant time in the development of the trans-Mississippi West. Established in 1859 by the United States Army as "Camp on Pawnee Fork," it guarded the eastern segment of the famed Santa Fe Trail, then the principal highway of commerce to the Southwest. A year later the Camp was relocated 4.8 km (3 miles) up the Pawnee River, and its name was changed to Fort Larned in honor of Colonel Benjamin F. Larned, Paymaster General of the Army.

The 1860 fort, despite misgivings of the builder, Major Henry Wessells, was constructed of sod and adobe. Later, beginning in 1865 and ending in 1868, more permanent buildings of native sandstone from nearby quarries, and pine brought in from the east, supplanted the earlier ones. Today the principal physical remains of the Fort consist of nine stone buildings in a quadrangle, all dating from 1867–68. They include two enlisted men's barracks, three buildings that housed officers, a shops building, two commissaries, and a quarter-master's building. All are in a remarkable state of preservation, although in various stages of stabilization and restoration.

Fort Larned, though abandoned only 18 years after its founding, effectively guarded the construction crews which pushed the Santa Fe Railroad westward across the Plains. The railroad displaced the slower, more vulnerable wagons, which for a long time had carried millions of dollars a year in commercial traffic between Independence, Missouri and Santa Fe. Upon completion of the railroad through central and western Kansas, Fort Larned was abandoned, in 1878.

As a military center Fort Larned served an important role in the Plains Indian War of 1863–64, and was the base for Major General Winfield Scott Hancock's expedition of 1867 against the Plains Indians. Throughout the 1860's the Fort was also an administrative center for attempts at peaceful dealings with these same Indians and from 1861 to 1868 officials of the Indian Bureau issued annuities here to the Cheyennes, Arapahos, Kiowas and Comanches in return for keeping the peace and staying away from Santa Fe rail traffic.

A few years after abandonment, the buildings and lands were sold at public auction and remained in private hands for 80 years. In 1964 the area was authorized as a National Historic Site by President Johnson.

At present there are no campgrounds or picnic areas, although a small campground and picnic spot, administered by the State of Kansas, is located .4 km (one quarter mile) from the Site's visitor center.

A detached area of 18 ha (44 acres) is located 8 km (5 miles) from the Fort quadrangle and contains some of the original Santa Fe Trail wagon ruts, and native prairie vegetation. Information about this unit may be obtained in the visitor center.

Inquiries concerning Fort Larned may be sent to the superintendent, Fort Larned National Historic Site, Route 3, Larned, Kansas 67550.

Fort Union
NEW MEXICO

The lure of high profits for American traders and a wider selection of merchandise at lower prices for New Mexicans resulted in mutually beneficial trade, beginning around 1821, on what later became known as the Santa Fe Trail. Twenty-five years of trade over this 1239 km (770 mile) economic link from Missouri to New Mexico made social and political ties as well. These, through combination with other factors in U.S.-Mexico relations, led to war between the two countries in 1846. The U.S. Army, channeling men and supplies over the Santa Fe Trail, reached Santa Fe in August. New Mexico was proclaimed part of the United States. At the end of the war, with signing of the Treaty of Guadalupe Hidalgo, General Kearney's 1846 proclamation became permanent. The treaty formally established a major new responsibility for American soldiers in New Mexico: to protect local inhabitants from the nomadic Indian tribes.

In 1851 the first Fort Union was established on the Santa Fe Trail, 153 km (95 miles) northeast of Santa Fe. On and off for the next ten years, Fort Union soldiers patrolled the area, helping to protect New Mexican citizens from the Jicarilla Apaches, Utes, Kiowas, and the Comanches. The early 1860's brought another major problem to Fort Union: the Civil War. At its outbreak many soldiers in New Mexico hurriedly left to join the Confederate Army. Soldiers remaining at the second Fort Union — built in 1861 — teamed with the Colorado Volunteers to repulse the Confederate Texans at the Battle of Glorieta Pass, saving New Mexico for the Union.

A third Fort Union, begun in 1863 and completed in 1869, became the largest supply depot in the southwest. While soldiers from Fort Union occasionally campaigned against outlaws, Indians, or comancheros, their main job, with civilians at the Fort, was forwarding supplies to other forts in the region. In 1879 the railroad reached Santa Fe, making the Santa Fe Trail obsolete; although Fort Union's main purpose for existence was gone, it stayed active on a very minor scale until 1891.

For many years the adobe ruins of Fort Union were unprotected, but in 1956 were included in a 292 ha (720 acre) National Park Service area authorized by Congress. Today, through continuing efforts of stabilization crews, visitors can walk a 2.4 km (1-½ mile) self-guided trail, viewing 30 ha (74 acres) of ruins, with the walls of some structures higher than 6 m (20 feet)! This self-guided trail is complete with interpretive signs, historic pictures in place, audio stations, taped bugle calls and retreat parade. In addition, during summer months, men and women park rangers will give talks and tours. Exhibits in the museum trace the story of military life in the southwest.

Fort Union is open daily, excepting Christmas and New Year; summer hours, 8 a.m.–7 p.m., winter hours, 8 a.m.–5 p.m. There are no camping facilities. For further information contact the superintendent at Fort Union National Monument, Watrous, New Mexico 87753 (1-505-425-8025).

31

Gila Cliff Dwellings
NEW MEXICO

Gila National Forest of southwestern New Mexico encompasses the spectacular canyon system of the East, West and Middle Forks of the Gila River. Within the Gila National Forest lies the Gila Wilderness, selected by the Forest Service in 1924 as the nation's first Wilderness.

The 216 ha (533 acre) Gila Cliff Dwellings National Monument, established in 1907, is on the eastern edge of the Gila Wilderness and easily accessible from Silver City. The visitor center is administered by the Forest Service under a cooperative agreement with the National Park Service. Forest Service personnel are responsible for protection and interpretation of the ruins at the National Monument. (Evening programs are given at an amphitheater during summer months.)

The National Monument is comprised of the Gila Cliff Dwellings and the TJ Site, two different types of settlements occupied in prehistoric times. The TJ Site was a sizeable pueblo in open country above the West Fork of the Gila. It has not been excavated and is closed to the public except by advance arrangement. The cliff dwellings were built in six natural caves in the southeast-facing cliff about 55 m (180 feet) above Cliff Dweller Canyon, a tributary of the West Fork. Both sites were occupied by Puebloan people who once lived in small pueblos and pithouses scattered throughout the area. The 40 cliff dwelling rooms were constructed in the 1280's by people of the Mogollon culture. Approximately 50 individuals lived in apartment-type stone houses built from Gila Conglomerate, in which the caves are located. The people were farmers; they raised corn, beans and squash in fields on mesa tops and along river bottoms. They hunted wild animals and gathered herbs, berries and nuts to supplement their crops. They had many crafts, including pottery and weaving. By the time Adolph Bandelier, prominent southwestern anthropologist, visited the caves in 1884, most of the artifacts had been removed by souvenir hunters. The National Park Service excavated the Cliff Dwellings in 1963.

By 1350 these people had abandoned their homes and fields. Why they left and where they went remains a mystery.

To see the cliff dwellings, park in the Monument parking area and follow the foot trail .8 km (½ mile) up Cliff Dweller Canyon and through the caves. The round-trip 1.6 km (1 mile) takes about one hour. All objects of antiquity and all animal and plant life are protected in the Monument, although fishing under New Mexico laws is permitted. No pets, please! Kennels are available at the Ranger Station.

The Monument and visitor center are open year round. Climate is warm, in mid-summer, with frequent thunderstorms; spring and fall are dry and sunny, with cool nights; mid-winter snows in canyons seldom last long, but persist in the high country. Campgrounds are located adjacent to the Monument.

Visitors wishing to know more about Gila National Forest, which ranges from semi-desert canyon bottoms at 1707 m (5,600 feet) to spruce-fir forests above 3048 m (10,000 feet) may get information from the Forest Supervisor, Gila National Forest, Silver City, New Mexico 88061.

Nearby facilities at Gila Hot Springs offer groceries, camping and picnicking supplies, gasoline, pack trips and a trailer court. For information on the Cliff Dwellings and adjacent Wilderness area, contact the District Ranger, Wilderness Ranger District, Route 11, Box 100, Silver City, New Mexico 88061.

Glen Canyon
ARIZONA — UTAH

Glen Canyon National Recreation Area extends from Grand Canyon, Arizona to Canyonlands National Park in Utah. Near Page, Arizona, Glen Canyon Dam retains the waters of Lake Powell, 177 m (580 feet) deep when full, 299 km (186 river miles) long. The canyon was named by Major John Wesley Powell, who led expeditions down the Green and Colorado Rivers in 1869 and 1871.

The dam and its 960,000 kw power plant, helping supply electricity for six states, were built by the Bureau of Reclamation. The recreation area is being developed by the National Park Service. Both cooperate with other state and federal agencies in managing specific aspects of the area.

Boating is Lake Powell's supreme attraction. Boating services, meals, lodging, campground, etc., are available year-round. The lake also attracts fishermen, chiefly seeking rainbow trout and large mouth bass, weighing up to 4.5 kg (10 pounds). Swimming is popular, but beginners should use only the sandy, gentle beaches. Deep waters between vertical walls are for experts only, and even they should observe two rules: never swim alone, and never swim from an unanchored boat. The only supervised beach at present is at Wahweap, near U.S. 89.

Other recreation centers are being developed at Bullfrog (reached from Hanksville, Utah), Halls Crossing (reached from Blanding and Mexican Hat), Lees Ferry (below the dam and reached from Marble Canyon, Arizona), and Hite (reached from Hanksville and Blanding). These will provide campgrounds, boat ramps, picnic areas, ranger stations, and concessioner-operated facilities such as restaurants, motels, trailer villages, boat services, etc.

The nearest town is Page, Arizona, elevation 1312 m (4,300 feet) with post office, bank, hospital, church, supermarket, and visitor facilities. Maximum temperatures in July and August average about 36C (96°F), with average minimum of 18C (65°). January and February minimums average −3C (26°), though temperature sometimes drops to −18C (zero) or below.

For several centuries the canyons were sparsely settled by Indians, probably seasonally, with most intensive occupation between A.D. 1000 and 1250. 1776 marked the first recorded visit, by Spanish Fathers Escalante and Dominguez, seeking a route to link Santa Fe with California missions.

Life forms are typical of semi-desert regions, save for waterfowl and fish. Whitetail antelope squirrels are common in daytime. Foxes, coyotes, and kangaroo rats appear mostly at night. Typical lizards are chuckwallas, horned and collared lizards. One dangerous reptile, the western rattlesnake, is found occasionally. You may see marsh hawks, sage sparrows, horned larks, and canyon wrens.

Common water-edge plants are tamarisk, willow, and cottonwood, with Utah juniper and pinyon at higher elevations. Attractive spring wildflowers begin blooming in April.

The rock formations are sediments, some deposited during invasions of ancient seas, some as windblown dunes. Navajo Sandstone cliffs at the dam reveal cross-sections of the latter. At Wahweap, the red, sea-deposited Carmel Formation overlies the Navajo Sandstone. Navajo Mountain was formed by molten rock pushing up into sedimentary layers, forming a huge rock dome. Erosion, wearing away uplifted sedimentary rocks, has yet to expose the once-molten core. A general uplift of the Colorado Plateau allowed slow-moving streams to speed up and cut winding canyons through layer after layer of colorful sediments.

The visitor center at Glen Canyon Bridge offers spectacular views of the dam, powerhouse, and canyon, and contains exhibits, a relief model of the entire recreation area, and an auditorium for frequent informational programs. Visitors may also take self guided tours through the dam and powerhouse.

Detailed information and maps are available from the superintendent, Glen Canyon National Recreation Area, P.O. Box 1507, Page, Arizona 86040.

Golden Spike

UTAH

Golden Spike National Historic Site was authorized as a unit of the National Park System in 1965 to commemorate the completion of the first transcontinental railroad. When the tracks of the Union Pacific and Central Pacific Railroads met at Promontory Summit, Utah, on May 10, 1869, a new era of history began.

Within a matter of months after introduction of the first steam locomotive to the United States, farsighted men conceived the idea of a railroad from the Atlantic to the Pacific. During several decades of debate on the subject, a railroad network spread over the East and the Midwest to the Mississippi River. A connecting link with the West Coast became a great public issue in the mid-19th century. Those who advocated the road foresaw its immediate economic benefits to the nation. Promise of a rail link to the East helped keep California in the Union during the Civil War, affecting the outcome of that conflict.

With the end of the Civil War came men and materials to push iron rails between Omaha, Nebraska and Sacramento, California. Four years, countless thousands of men, and untold millions of money went into the effort. It was a struggle that combined political and economic forces; united moguls, financiers, engineers, and laborers; brought together Americans, Europeans, and Orientals, freeborn and ex-slave. Deserts, prairies, and mountains were crossed, each mile yielding grudgingly before the onslaught. In the end 2858 km (1776 miles) of track were laid to unite East with West and make of the United States one nation.

Clearly a great deal of American history is reflected at Golden Spike National Historic Site. That last spike of gold symbolized half a century of sentiment for a Pacific Railroad and marked the beginning of the end of the Great Plains frontier. Neither the blizzards of winter nor the searing heat of summer can erase the significance of that climactic moment when the Golden Spike sank home.

Located north of the Great Salt Lake and 48 km (30 miles) west of Brigham City, this National Historic Site includes the Golden Spike Site itself and significant remains of the Union and Central Pacific grades where they crossed the Promontory mountains.

On May 10, 1969, the centennial anniversary of the completion of the railroad, the National Park Service dedicated a quarter-million dollar visitor center to interpret the story of the building of the railroad and its impact on our nation's history. There is much to capture the imagination as one contemplates the dramatic and jubilant moment in the nation's youth when the "greatest railroad on earth" was completed. The building houses exhibits, information and sales counter, and an auditorium. A twenty minute color movie depicting the building of the Transcontinental Railroad is shown in the auditorium. A paved path leads from the building to the spot where the May 10, 1869, ceremony is re-enacted 4 times a day during the summer to recreate the living historic scene of that time.

Like the echo of the old steam engine the iron trail over the Promontory Mountains lives only in memory. But it can live again as you traverse 15 miles of the historic construction scene in your own vehicle and by hiking. The tour naturally falls into three parts: a 24 km (15 mile) round trip to the west and two detours off the pavement to the east on your way back to Highway 83.

For additional information contact the superintendent, Golden Spike National Historic Site, Box 394, Brigham City, Utah 84302.

Grand Canyon National Park

ARIZONA

Adequate description is impossible. When you haven't seen the Grand Canyon, you can't imagine it; when you have, printed words fail you! For perhaps 6 million years the Colorado has been digging its chasm in an elevated section of the earth's crust. It winds 446 km (277 miles) through the 4931 sq km (1904 square miles) of park. A National Monument in 1908, a National Park since 1919, the area now includes the former Grand Canyon and Marble Canyon National Monuments.

The 2135 m (7,000 foot) altitudinal range illustrates climate progression from canyon bottom Mexican desert to that of southern Canada on the North Rim. The pine-forested South Rim, 2135 m (7,000 feet) above sea level, open the year round, has Park headquarters and Grand Canyon Village. The colder North Rim, 344 km (214 miles) away by road and 305 m to 610 m (1,000 to 2,000 feet) higher, is closed usually from mid-October to mid-May.

South Rim accommodations and services range from campgrounds to hotel suites. There are Park Service campgrounds (in summer normally filled before 10:00 a.m.) with tables, fireplaces, water and restrooms, at the Village and Desert View, and concessioner-sold firewood. Trailer Village, near the visitor center, has utility hookups. Hotels fill early in summer, so for rates and reservations write Fred Harvey, Grand Canyon, Arizona, quite early in the season. There is a medical clinic, post office, bank, kennel, service station, garage and general store with supermarket.

North Rim has a Park Service campground with tables, fireplaces, wood, running water and restrooms.

Bright Angel Point has a gas station and grocery. For rates and reservations at Grand Canyon Lodge and North Rim Inn, write: T.W.A. Services, Inc., P.O. Box 400, Cedar City, Utah 84720.

Grand Canyon's rich and varied interpretive program includes auto rim drives; the 2.4 km (1½ mile) Canyon Rim Nature Trail from the hotel to the visitor center and Yavapai Museum; hiking trails; lectures at West Rim points (summer); Tusayan Ruin and Museum (summer); and illustrated evening talks at the Village (summer) and visitor center amphitheatres. During the summer there is a free bus system operating in the South Rim Village and along the West Rim Drive, which is closed to private vehicles from about April to September. Concessioner operated bus drives and mule trips into the Canyon are popular. For mule trips, advance reservations are essential. Write to: Fred Harvey, Grand Canyon, Arizona 86023. Colorado River raft trips are available. For a list of companies, write the Park superintendent. On the North Rim geology talks are given each afternoon at Cape Royal, with evening programs at the campground and in the Lodge. There are leisurely conducted nature walks along the Transept Trail, as well as hiking trails. Other nature trails include one at Tusayan Ruins and one near Phantom Ranch. Check with Park Service employees for safety rules, before taking hikes. Camping below the rim, and hiking off main trails, is by permit only.

For back country campground reservations and information, call 638-2474 or write the Park superintendent.

Grand Canyon (Tuweep Unit)
ARIZONA

This area *was* Grand Canyon National Monument from 1932 to 1974, and covered about 806 sq km (310 square miles) of primitive area between Lake Mead National Recreation Area and Grand Canyon National Park. In January of 1975 it became the *Tuweep Unit* of the latter.

The geology here is similar to that upstream, but adds a more recent chapter of volcanic activity. After the principal topographic features of the region had developed and the side canyons had cut nearly down to their present level, great quantities of molten lava poured forth from at least 60 volcanic craters. The lava built the Pine Mountain range — about 48 km (30 miles) long — and flowed down the north wall of Grand Canyon, damming old Toroweap Canyon and the Colorado River. Waters behind the Toroweap's lava dam weren't strong enough to cut the barrier away, so they dropped their silt. Eventually, fill accumulated to a depth of about 1610 m (2000 feet), creating today's Toroweap Valley.

The waters of the main river channel, also dammed into a great lake, were too powerful to be retained; they overflowed and with sandy silt finally "sandpapered" the lava dam away. Remains of this dam may yet be seen on both sides of the Colorado in the Inner Gorge.

A park ranger is on duty at the Tuweep Ranger Station the year round, and water is available only in event of an emergency, but there is no lodging or meals. South of the station near the Rim is a small campground. It is not advisable for anyone to attempt a trip to the Monument without ample gasoline, water, food, camp outfit, and tools.

After passing the ranger station, an unimproved road leads on for 10 km (6 miles) to the brink of Grand Canyon at Toroweap Point, one of the most breathtaking spectacles in the entire length of Grand Canyon. Here the Canyon is less than 1.6 km (a mile) wide, and you look straight down the sheer rock walls to the snakelike shimmer of the Colorado, 915 m (3,000 feet) below. On quiet days you hear the background roar of Lava Falls Rapids and sense the incredible power they represent. To the west is Mount Trumbull, elevation 2449 m (8,028 feet) above sea level, the last landmark on the western horizon of the Grand Canyon country.

For more information, write to the superintendent, Grand Canyon National Park 86023.

Gran Quivira

NEW MEXICO

In the central highlands of New Mexico, 2013 m (6,600 feet) above sea level, and 40 km (25 miles) south of Mountainair, is the 247 ha (611-acre) Gran Quivira National Monument, established in 1909 to preserve the ruins of two 17th Century Spanish missions and the Piro Indian pueblo of Las Humanas. These structures represent the contact period of Spanish and Indian cultures in the Southwest, at which time cultural exchange, conflict, and rejection were actively operating toward the explosive Pueblo Rebellion of 1680.

By 1530 the Spanish frontier in the New World was just south of the present United States-Mexico boundary. Tales of vast wealth to the north circulated in Mexico City and the spirit of riches-through-conquest prevailed.

The expeditions of Coronado (1540), Rodriquez-Chamuscado (1581), Espejo (1582), and Sosa (1590) all missed Gran Quivira. Don Juan Oñate's expedition of 1598 established the first colony in New Mexico, and in October of that year he visited this Piro pueblo, one of several in the region. The Piros, who had a hunting-gathering-farming economy, also carried on considerable trade with the tribes on the plains and gathered salt from nearby brackish lakes as an item to trade with other pueblos, an activity which the Spaniards capitalized on in the middle 1600's.

Spanish historical documents provide a fragmentary glimpse of mission life at Las Humanas (Gran Quivira) during the 17th Century. In 1626 the pueblo was a **visita,** or visiting place of the Franciscan mission of San Gregorio at the Piro Pueblo of Abo, 32 km (20 miles) to the northwest. Between 1629 and 1631 Fray Francisco de Letrado directed the building of the first mission church at Las Humanas. It was a small, rectangular structure dedicated to San Isidro. For 28 years thereafter, the town was again a **visita** of Abo.

In 1659 Fray Diego de Santander, a newly assigned father, was reported working on San Buenaventura mission, a massive cruciform church and convento which enclosed more than 1620 sq m (18,000 square feet) with exterior walls 1.8 m (6 feet) thick at the base. Labors of the Indians on this mission continued until 1669, when the missionary father left. Severe drought and associated pestilence, the burden of the Spanish **repartimiento** (a form of conscripted labor), and increasingly severe raids by Apache Indians to the east caused the villagers in the early 1670's to abandon their centuries-old village and join relatives in the Rio Grande valley near present-day Socorro.

The visitor center is open daily, and you should see its exhibits on archeology and history before taking the self-guiding walk along the Mission Trail. Ranger guided tours are usually available for organized groups, all year round. There is a picnic ground, but no facilities for overnight camping. Address of the resident superintendent is Route 1, Mountainair, New Mexico 87036.

Great Sand Dunes

COLORADO

At the eastern edge of the San Luis Valley in south-central Colorado, paralleling for nearly 16 km (10 miles) the base of the heavily forested snowcapped Sangre de Cristo Mountains, are some of the highest inland sand dunes in the United States. Their wind-tossed curling crests rise to almost 214 m (700 feet) above the valley floor, dwarfing the cottonwood trees which line the banks of adjacent Medano Creek. Bordering the great valley are the Sangre de Cristos to east and northeast, towering to over 4270 m (14,000 feet) above sea level; the San Juans to the west; and the San Luis hills to the south. Fed by melting snow, streams have carried sand, silt, and gravel down from the mountains into the valley for thousands of years, and most of them drop their loads and sink into the valley floor a short distance from the mountains.

The prevailing southwesterly winds, sand-laden, sweep across the valley and funnel through the lowest gaps in the Sangre de Cristos. In rising to reach the passes the winds lose much velocity, and drop their sand burden at the foot, a natural trap. Here the dunes have formed. And here the dunes and Medano Creek, at the meeting place of valley floor and mountain range, provide a variety of altitudinal and climatic conditions which require considerable adaptation by plants and animals to the dunes and their fringe areas.

Ancient campsites reveal that Folsom Man roamed the region about 10,000 years ago, and after him various other primitive peoples. In fairly recent times the valley was controlled by the Ute Indians, who made it their permanent home. Spanish explorers reached the valley in 1779, when Juan Bautista de Anza returned this way from a punitive expedition against the Comanches. In the winter of 1806–7, Lieutenant Zebulon Pike's expedition came through, followed by later explorers and finally settlers in the early 1850's.

In 1932 a 143 sq km (55-square-mile) area of dunes and nearby wild country was established as a National Monument, and a superintendent is now in charge. His address is Box 60, Alamosa, Colorado 81101.

In summer, provisions and gasoline may be obtained at the Great Sand Dunes Company immediately south of the monument or at the Dunes Outpost 1.6 km (one mile) south of the boundary. They can be purchased all year at Mosca 40 km (25 miles) to the west and Alamosa 60 km (37 miles) southwest. Within the monument accommodations are limited to the 88 unit Pinyon Flat Campground, with wood, water, tables, fireplaces, and restrooms, and a picnic area near the dunes. Campground space cannot be reserved, so the policy is "first come, first served."

Your first stop should be at the visitor center, where exhibits explain the natural history, prehistory, and history. Afterward, you are better informed and can enjoy the dunes more.

The Montville Trail provides an enjoyable half-hour stroll through a small valley, with trailside features explained in a leaflet which you obtain at the visitor center.

Photography on the dunes is best in early morning or late afternoon. Camera settings should be similar to those for beach or snow scenes.

The best sand impressions, telling night's story of animal and insect activity, with tracery formed by wind-blown plants, are found in early morning.

Guadalupe Mountains

TEXAS

The Guadalupe mountains of New Mexico and Texas consist of Permian marine limestone and are probably the most extensive fossil reef on earth. They contain Carlsbad Caverns National Park, described elsewhere, and the recently established Guadalupe Mountains National Park. First considered for inclusion in the National Park System in the early 1930's, title to some of the area's most beautiful canyon country was donated to the Government in 1961. Since then, through donation, exchange and purchase, virtually all the 333 sq km (128 square miles) of mountain wilderness and Chihuahuan desert has been acquired.

The four highest peaks in Texas are in the Park. From the tallest, Guadalupe 2669 m (8,751 feet) above sea level, the others, Shumard, Bartlett and Bush Mountain, extend NNW within a scant 4.8 km (3-mile) distance of one another in a nearly straight line.

From the base of the western escarpment, at 1122 m (3,680 feet) above sea level, to the peak tops, are life zones from Lower Sonoran into Canadian. Vegetation typifies Chihuahuan deserts, canyon hardwoods, and highland evergreen forests of Ponderosa, limber pine, and Douglas-fir. Animal life includes elk, mule deer, turkey, coyote, ringtail, raccoon, porcupine and bobcat, with an occasional mountain lion or black bear.

Ecologically the park is a jewel, having numerous relict and rare plant associations. Because of the fragile natural balance here, the most famous canyon, McKittrick, is open only to day-use foot travel. Arrangements must be made at Frijole Information Station for this relatively level hike.

Major public use facilities have not yet been constructed. Some provisions for visitor enjoyment are near U.S. Highway 62-180, which crosses the southeast edge and provides spectacular views of the 1610 m (2,000 foot) sheer cliff El Capitan, Guadalupe Peak, and the mountain range. Roadside picnic areas have been provided by the state of Texas.

There is a small, primitive campground, with tables, trash cans, and chemical toilets, in Pine Spring Canyon, near Pine Springs Camp, Texas. Only containerized fuels are permitted. No wood gathering is allowed. Drinking water is available at Frijole Information Station.

The 101 km (63 miles) of hiking trails are primitive, steep, and marked only with rock cairns. With no source of drinking water, hikers must carry their own on backcountry trips. For these backpack campers there are eight campsites. All hikers are requested to check in and out by signing a register at Frijole Information Station or Pine Springs Canyon campground. Overnight trips require a backcountry permit, available at the information station. Hikers must pack out all refuse. Open fires are not permitted.

The mountain country is a rugged framework of sedimentary limestone, which makes rock climbing hazardous. There is additional danger of becoming lost, injured or stranded. Weather conditions can change drastically in the microclimate so that high winds, fire, hypothermia, and heat exhaustion are real dangers. This backcountry is not for the frail or the uninformed!

The usual essential Park Service regulations apply here: No littering, no hunting or molesting wildlife, no firearms, no prospecting, no collecting, and pets must be on leash or otherwise under physical restraint at all times.

The park is administered by a superintendent, whose address is 3225 National Parks Highway, Carlsbad, New Mexico 88220.

Hovenweep

UTAH-COLORADO

Astride the Utah-Colorado line is the 204 ha (504-acre) Hovenweep National Monument, established in 1923 to preserve several groups of prehistoric Pueblo Indian ruins. Here are the famous square, oval, circular, and D-shaped masonry towers, probably the best-preserved examples of this type of architecture in the Southwest. Four of the six ruins clusters are in Colorado and two in Utah, the Square Tower Canyon group being the largest and best preserved.

The structures were built of native sandstone blocks, quarried and shaped by Indian builders. Most towers are at the heads of small draws or box canyons, sometimes atop great blocks of fallen rimrock. Most are located near small springs or water conserving farming terraces, suggesting that they may have been ceremonial innovations, attempts to counter effects of increasing aridity in the 1100's and 1200's.

The culture of the Hovenweep people was similar to that of the Indians who lived in what is now Mesa Verde National Park. Descendants are among present-day Pueblo Indians of New Mexico and Arizona. When the Indians of the San Juan region adopted farming practices at least 2,000 years ago, they began to settle down, at first living in shallow caves. Later they learned to build crude pithouses and then mud surface houses with walls reinforced with timbers, which in the 900's, were replaced by stone masonry pueblos.

These people raised corn, beans, and squash, supplemented these crops with edible wild plants, domesticated the turkey, and hunted and trapped birds and wild animals. Each family produced its own items of household and personal needs, often decorating their products with attractive, artistic designs.

During the period of A.D. 1100–1300 the Pueblo people of Hovenweep withdrew from small sites in open valleys and mesa tops and concentrated near canyon heads. Here they built dams to store water, large compact pueblos, and tall towers still standing today. The long draws below the dams could be terraced for farming and furnished with water collected behind the dams during rains. The severe drought of 1276 to 1299 brought hardship to these people, and they drifted southward to the Rio Grande and Little Colorado drainages, never to return.

Today Hovenweep lacks food and lodging, stores, service stations or paved roads, but does have a 31-site campground with drinking water, although firewood is not available. Roads are fair except during and immediately after storms. The park staff is headquartered the year-round at Square Tower Group, although inquiries should be addressed to: Superintendent, Mesa Verde National Park, Colorado 81330, or Hovenweep National Monument, McElmo Route, Cortez, Colorado 81321.

Hubbell Trading Post

ARIZONA

The Hubbell Trading Post, founded about 1876 and operated by Don Lorenzo Hubbell after about 1878, stands as the last of a trading empire that lasted for nearly a century. The trading post and its surrounding land is significant in the preservation today of trading posts of yesterday. Because of its historical integrity, its continuity of operation, and the history of its founder, it is the best sample to portray this little known, forgotten or misunderstood part of our American history. Thus the area was created by Congress as a national historic site in 1965, and transferred to the National Park system on April 3, 1967.

The Hubbell home richly portrays the history of the Southwest, and the pattern of life shaped and enjoyed by the trader himself. Hand-crafted products of many Indian tribes, and paintings by many famous artists, adorn the walls throughout.

Guided tours through the old trading post and grounds, and the Hubbell home, in effect enable visitors to turn back the hands of time to the beginning of this century. The trading post still operates, under management by Southwest Parks and Monuments Association, in much the same manner as it has done for several generations.

Located in the heart of the colorful Navajo Indian Reservation in Northeastern Arizona, at an elevation of 1983 m (6,500 feet) above sea level, the area is 1.6 km (one mile) west of the town of Ganado. This altitude produces rugged winter weather at times, with oc-

casional heavy snow, usually of short duration. Summer days are warm to hot, and the nights are cool.

These semi-arid uplands support a scattered growth of pinyons and junipers, interspersed with such plants as sagebrush, saltbush, rabbitbrush, cactus, yucca, and annual and perennial herbs such as beeweed, sunflower, snakeweed, and four-o'clock.

All-weather roads lead from the four points of the compass, with such attractions as Petrified Forest National Park, Canyon de Chelly National Monument, and many Tribal areas, less than a day away. The visitor is wise to remember in this region that there are non-graded side roads leading to many places in the Reservation, on which it is possible for strangers to get lost, or stuck in slippery places during the rainy periods. The area is open to visitation during all 12 months of the year.

Overnight tourist facilities are lacking in the immediate neighborhood (1978), although the town of Ganado has a cafe, stores, and service stations. Motel accommodations occur at Window Rock, the Navajo Indian Capitol, and ample overnight facilities and businesses of many kinds exist in Gallup, 87 km (54 miles) east, known throughout the nation as a major Indian trading center.

For information about Hubbell Trading Post National Historic Site you can write to the superintendent in immediate charge of the area whose address is Box 150, Ganado, Arizona, 86505.

Lake Mead

NEVADA — ARIZONA

Lake Mead National Recreation Area consists of over 7020 sq km (2,700 square miles) of lakes, canyons, plateaus, and colorful desert wilderness in Arizona and Nevada, extending to Grand Canyon National Park on the east to Davis Dam on the south. Altitudes range from 158 m (517 feet) above sea level on the Colorado River below Davis Dam to 2132 m (6,990 feet) atop Mt. Dellenbaugh on the Shivwits Plateau. Hoover Dam, retaining Lake Mead, rises 222 m (726.4 feet). The Bureau of Reclamation began construction of the dam in 1931, and the structure was dedicated in 1935.

This is a recreation area, a place for outdoor activity, boating, fishing, water-skiing, camping, swimming, picnicking, exploring, and scenic desert drives. It is also a place for relaxation. The two lakes, Mead and Mohave, with surface capacity of 712 sq km (274 square miles) and 1448 km (900 miles) of shoreline, offer settings ranging from mountain-framed basins to secluded, shadowed coves, from wide sandy beaches to spectacular canyon walls.

Most of the recreation area is desert land of less than 15 cm (6 inches) annual rainfall. But desert does not mean deserted. Plants abound, unique, highly specialized ones that lie dormant during summer heat, awaiting only winter rains to explode into a procession of wildflowers from February to June.

Animals too, have adapted. Over 60 species of mammals live here, from the majestic desert bighorn sheep and shaggy wild burros to the coyotes, foxes, badgers, bobcats, and ring-tails. Mountain lions and mule deer roam the higher eastern plateaus, and small rodents abound everywhere. The lakes have a variety of introduced game species, such as the rainbow trout, catfish and largemouth black bass. The water also attracts a parade of birds ranging from hummingbirds to eagles, with over 250 species having been reported from the area. The desert also has its share of lizards and snakes.

Man has also left his mark. Trails, campsites, and petroglyphs represent desert dwellers who once roamed in northern Arizona and Nevada. Village ruins along the Virgin River represent another people, marginal farmers who traded with Great Basin neighbors to the north and were strongly influenced by Pueblo Indians of northeastern Arizona. In the 1100's, a Great Basin group, ancestral to the Shoshonean nomads, moved in, and the farmers then drifted eastward to merge with their Puebloan friends.

Long afterward came the miners whose abandoned workings and ghost towns still dot the desert. Mighty Hoover Dam climaxed this story in 1935, followed by Davis Dam in 1952.

The Recreation Area is open all year; however the weather is most pleasant from late September through early December and from early February through late May.

There are many scheduled activities. Bureau of Reclamation guides conduct daily tours through Hoover Dam from 8:30 to 4:15; self-guiding tours are available at Davis Dam.

Tape recorder tour and a guided boat trip are offered. Exhibits explaining the features of the area are displayed at various developed centers around the lakes. Concessioners provide other services, including boat tours on Lake Mead.

For information on how best to enjoy the area safely, write to the superintendent, Lake Mead National Recreation Area, 601 Nevada Highway, Boulder City, Nevada 89005.

Lake Meredith

TEXAS

Lake Meredith is the national recreation area behind Sanford Dam, about 64 km (40 miles) northeast of Amarillo. This is a land of cattle and natural gas refineries, on the dry, windswept Llano Estacado (staked plains), the High Plains of the Texas Panhandle. Across the Llano, one of the so-called flattest places on earth, the Canadian River has patiently cut the 60 meter (200 foot) deep canyons now being filled in by the 32 km (20 miles) of lake and its 161 km (100 plus miles) of shoreline. The maximum conservation pool elevation will be 896 m (2937 feet) above sea level.

The Bureau of Reclamation built the dam, primarily to store water for municipal and industrial use by 11 Texas cities, under a 50-year repayment contract. By co-operative inter bureau agreement the National Park Service administers the recreation area.

The sparkling oasis of Lake Meredith can fill a week-end or longer visit with fun, exercise, and relaxation. Water activities include boating, water skiing, sailing, swimming and scuba diving. You may picnic, camp, study nature, or just enjoy sightseeing. Special events, such as dune buggy and motorcycle races are held by local groups.

Hunting and fishing are regulated by the state of Texas in cooperation with the National Park Service, with Texas fishing licenses required. Wildlife includes a few whitetail and mule deer, pronghorns, rabbits, skunks, and ground squirrels. There are waterfowl such as geese and ducks, quail, doves and turkeys.

Some portions of the area are open to hunting in season. Fishermen may seek walleye, as well as large and small mouth bass, white bass, four species of catfish, crappie, sunfish and carp.

All persons boating or otherwise using the lake should be extremely conscious of the speed with which violent windstorms, especially in spring time, can arise. Boaters should know in advance of locations of sheltered coves in which they may wait out these winds.

Man has lived on the Llano Estacado, attempting to cope with the harsh environment, for approximately 12,000 years, and traces of prehistoric Indian homes, workshops and campsites dot the entire Canadian River system. Here temperatures may range from a summer high of 40C (105°) down to a shivery −23C (minus 10°) in winter, with about 35 cm (14 inches) of snow a year and total precipitation around 52 cm (21 inches).

Anti pollution requirements for Lake Meredith are, of necessity, rigid. There are ample designated disposal stations for waste. Information about such requirements, and regulations on safe boating management, should be obtained before entering the area, at park headquarters in Fritch. Here also visits to Alibates National Monument's flint quarries may be arranged for, as well as at the Bates Canyon Information Station.

For further information on Lake Meredith address the superintendent of the area at P.O. Box 1438, Fritch, Texas 79036.

43

Travelers who have crossed vast stretches of desert in the Great Basin find the sudden transition of climate and vegetation at Lehman Caves National Monument a surprising and welcome change. The Monument, nearly 2,135 m (7,000 feet) above sea level, is within the upper reaches of the desert and in the pinyon pine and juniper zone of vegetation. The impressive ridge of Wheeler Peak, at 3,984 m (13,063 feet), is the second highest in Nevada and provides the background to the west. One can look eastward across a vast expanse of desert, interrupted by rugged mountains of the Basin and Range province.

These pleasant surroundings and dramatic views are bonuses. Visitors usually come to visit the underground wilderness for which the Monument was established. Within the rooms and along the .9 km (6/10 mile) of paved trail through Lehman Caves are myriads of delicate and intricate cave formations, including dozens of the rare and puzzling shields or "palettes." Twisting helictites, which defy gravity in their growth pattern, along with cave coral or popcorn and frosty incrustations grow on many of the formations and cover walls and ceilings where other forms of decorations do not occur. Also the delicate crystals of Aragonite, first discovered in a cave in Spain, are found in at least two places in the cave. Seeing the incredible beauty of the cave with indirect lighting is an absorbing and emotional experience. An appreciation for the geologic processes which produced the scene through millions of years is fostered by observing one of the keys to the past, present and future of the cave — drops of water falling occasionally and adding a minute bit of calcite to a formation.

Reputedly discovered in the spring of 1885 by Absalom Leman, a pioneer homesteader, who settled below the Monument in the late 1860's, the cave was partially explored and developed by the turn of the century. Early visitors often left initials or names smoked on the walls and ceilings and broke numerous formations for souvenirs or to crawl through some of the narrow passageways, apparently not realizing or caring that this damage would probably never be repaired. Yet, the cave today is in better condition than most that are open to visitation.

Lehman Caves
NEVADA

The area was established as a National Monument by proclamation of President Harding in 1922, and for 11 years was administered by the Forest Service. An executive order in 1933 assigned responsibility to the National Park Service, and a resident custodian was appointed. The Monument now embraces 259 ha (640 acres) which is entirely surrounded by Humboldt National Forest.

The cave is chilly, so warm clothing is recommended for the 1½ hour conducted trips, given daily. The Park Service maintains picnic facilities (no camping) in the headquarters area. A concessioner sells refreshments and meals from April through October. Several campgrounds are available in the adjacent National Forest. The mailing address of the Lehman Caves superintendent is Baker, Nevada 89311.

Lyndon B. Johnson
TEXAS

Lyndon B. Johnson National Historic Site, situated in the Hill Country of south central Texas, is unique among presidential parks and landmarks in the United States, for within its boundaries are historic sites and structures representing origins, ancestry and full life cycle of a president who was first, last and always a product of his native land and human environment. It is essential to see the country to see the man.

The region is dominated by low, rugged hills covered by gnarled live oak trees and chaparral. Scattered rock outcroppings, clear streams, peaceful farmlands and historic towns round out a picture which did much to shape the L.B.J. character into a toughness, gentleness and resiliency so essential to his career. Here was the union between harsh, high plains, plateaus and deserts of the west with gentle streams, small valleys and fat cattle underneath ragged skylines of rock and juniper.

At times this area along the Pedernales River is incredibly beautiful and suggestive of all the peace and harmony in nature. At other times, blizzards howl in from the plains, heat and drowth strike viciously, and summer storms sweep violently through the hills, battering with hail and ripping valleys with cloudburst floods.

The park has two distinct areas: Johnson City, and the L.B.J. Ranch, 22 km (14 miles) apart. The former contains the Boyhood Home of L.B.J. and the nearby Johnson Settlement, and a visitor center which provides exhibits and park information. Johnson City was where Lyndon did most of his growing up.

At the L.B.J. Ranch area you arrive first at the L.B.J. State Park Visitor Center, from which Park Service buses depart for the ranch tour, including the one-room country school attended by Lyndon at the age of four, his birthplace, the family cemetery where President Johnson is buried, and the ranch with its registered Hereford cattle.

At the Boyhood Home in Johnson City you may walk or take an old-fashioned wagon ride to nearby Johnson Settlement, a complex of restored historic structures tracing evolution of the Hill Country from open-range cattle kingdom days of L.B.J.'s grandfather, Sam Ealy Johnson, Sr., to the later local ranching and farming. You can show the kids longhorn cattle here, and can remember what you've read and heard about the old-time cattle drovers, and "up the Chisholm Trail" to Abilene, Kansas, in the 1860's and 1870's.

For additional information, write the park superintendent, whose address is: National Park Service, P.O. Box 329, Johnson City, Texas 78636. This office can also give you information on nearby Fredericksburg and its Admiral Nimitz Museum, and the Lyndon Baines Johnson Library, on the campus of the University of Texas at Austin, operated by the National Archives and Records Service.

Mesa Verde

COLORADO

Established in 1906, Mesa Verde is our only national park devoted primarily to prehistoric cliff dwellings and related works of early man. Its 208 sq km (80 square miles) of high mesa country are located in extreme southwestern Colorado, on U.S. 160, midway between the towns of Cortez and Mancos. From the Park entrance 34 km (20 miles) of all-weather mountainous road lead to Park headquarters and the major attractions. Here a culture designated by archeologists as the Anasazi (a Navajo word meaning "ancient ones") developed from the first evidence of occupancy in the last half of the 6th century. This resulted in the greatest concentration of cliff dwelling communities in the Southwest.

The Anasazi achieved an advanced sedentary culture raising crops of corn, beans, and squash on the mesa tops. They began building pithouses, making pottery and baskets, and domesticating turkeys and dogs. Between A.D. 750 and 1100 they lived in small masonry pueblos near their farmlands and adopted new craft techniques and art styles from neighboring groups to the south.

The Classic period (A.D. 100 to 1300) is represented by huge structures such as Cliff Palace, largest and most famous cliff dwelling in the United States. Not until the early 1200's did the Anasazi gradually leave mesa and valley pueblos and move to cave or cliff locations or sites near heads of canyons. A combination of environmental factors, including drought from A.D. 1276 to 1299 and general depletion of natural resources (soil, forest cover, and game animals) brought about complete abandonment. Emigrants probably moved east and south, joining other Pueblo people along the Rio Grande drainage.

Today Park visitors can travel a loop road drive to surface ruins showing the entire range of local prehistoric architectural development, where different sites reveal construction sequence from early to late. Mesa top pueblos were most numerous, although cliff dwellings were more dramatic, especially Spruce Tree House, one of the best preserved dwellings.

You enter the Park at about 2135 m (7000 feet) elevation, along a ridge separating two valleys. At Park Point on the north rim is the highest elevation 2614 m (8572 feet) and a panoramic view of the Four Corners region. The pinyon-juniper forested mesa gives way at higher levels to dense stands of scrub oak, mountain mahogany, fendlerbush, serviceberry, small amounts of Douglas-fir and Rocky Mountain juniper, and occasional quaking aspens and Ponderosa pines. Flowering shrubs glorify the spring, and wildflowers bloom from early spring to late autumn, with best autumn coloring in late September.

Over 170 species of birds and 50 species of mammals have been recorded, including the common mule deer, bobcats, coyotes, gray foxes, chipmunks, rock squirrels, and rarely a black bear or mountain lion. Reintroduced, bighorn sheep are sometimes seen.

The Park is open year round, but the best visitor time is early May to October 15, when interpretive activities, accommodations, and other services are available. During the remainder of the year lodging, meals, groceries, and gas are not available. Ranger-guided trips are conducted to Spruce Tree House throughout the year, weather permitting, and the Museum and Mesa Top road loop are also open.

Upon arrival in summer you should go first to the Far View Visitor Center for orientation and aid in planning your visit, which can include a bus trip out to Wetherill Mesa and other varied activities. For advance information write the Superintendent, Mesa Verde National Park, Colorado 81330.

Montezuma Castle

ARIZONA

High in a limestone cliff recess on Beaver Creek, in the Verde Valley of central Arizona, is Montezuma Castle, one of the most interesting and best preserved cliff dwellings in the United States. Early settlers named it on the erroneous assumption that Aztecs fleeing the Spanish conquest in Mexico built here. A bare 91 m (100 yards) farther west, in a larger and shallower cliff hollow, are the remnants of a much larger, contemporary cliff village, which burned and collapsed centuries ago. This structure, known as "Castle A," was excavated in 1933–34 and some of the artifacts that were found are on display in the visitor center.

The builders of the Castle, a 20-room, 5-story apartment house, were Sinaguas, dry-farming Pueblo Indians who drifted into the fertile valley from the plateau to the north in the 12th century. For a while they apparently lived harmoniously with the Hohokam, who had come from the south about 400 years earlier and who irrigated and farmed the stream terraces while living in one-room pole-and-brush house clusters. The Sinagua adopted Hohokam irrigation, and the latter seem to have borrowed masonry architecture from them. Before long, Sinagua culture dominated, although partly reshaped by Hohokam contacts and the new environment.

Long droughts in the late 1200's brought many more Sinaguan immigrants from the Flagstaff region, undoubtedly causing over-crowding of the central portion of the valley. The combination of too many people and not enough farmland may be crucial in explaining the general population decline which occurred through the early 1400's. By 1450 Montezuma Castle appears to

have been completely abandoned. Although it is uncertain where they went, some groups of the present Hopi Indians from Northern Arizona claim partial descent from the Sinagua.

Montezuma Well, 11 km (7 miles) northeast of the Castle, is a large limestone sink containing a small lake from which flows 5,700,000 liters (1,500,000 gallons) of water a day. Indians built cliff and hilltop houses around the Well and diverted its lime-charged waters through ditches to irrigate crops. The lime settled and hardened, cementing and preserving some ditch portions perfectly. The story of the people is similar to that at the Castle.

Your first stop at the Castle will be at the visitor center where the exhibits will help you understand the things you will see when you follow the self-guiding trail to the ruins. Due to the fragile nature of the 700 year old dwelling and for the safety of visitors, entrance into Montezuma Castle is not permitted. However, visitors may explore the excavated lower rooms of "Castle A," including a natural cave room.

There is a large picnic area at Montezuma Well, with cooking permitted and fireplaces provided, and a smaller "cold-lunch" picnic area near the Castle. The U.S. Forest Service maintains ample camping facilities in Oak Creek Canyon and at nearby Clear and Beaver Creeks. Motels, grocery stores and restaurants are available in Camp Verde, 18 km (5 miles) south of the Castle, where also is located the historic Fort Verde Museum.

Montezuma Castle was established as a National Monument in 1906 and contains 341 hectares (842 acres). This includes the Well as a detached section. The Monument is located along Interstate 17, 80 km (50 miles) south of Flagstaff and 145 km (90 miles) north of Phoenix.

For further information contact the superintendent, Montezuma Castle National Monument, P.O. Box 219, Camp Verde, Arizona 86322.

Natural Bridges

UTAH

San Juan County, in southeastern Utah, is a land of brilliantly colored cliffs, winding box canyons, sandstone pinnacles and arches, and pinyon-and-juniper clad hills. Near the center of this region are the three huge natural bridges of the 3078 ha (7,600 acre) National Monument, established in 1908. The highest is Sipapu, 67 m (220 feet) high, with a spanning 82 m (268 feet); next is Kachina, 64 m (210 feet) high with a 63 m (206 foot) span; and finally, Owachoma, 32 m (106 feet) high, spanning 55 m (180 feet). A 14 km (9-mile) loop road affords excellent views into the canyons and the 3 bridges. Trails are available to take short walks into the canyons for a close-up look at the bridges.

The bridges occur in crossbedded Cedar Mesa Sandstone, in two deep and meandering canyons. Streams, especially desert-type ones which occasionally scour their rocky bottoms and walls with a tremendous head of water and sand, always seek to make a straight channel with an even grade. During floods, silt-laden water grinds with great force against meander walls, occasionally working a hole through a long-standing fin of rock around which the stream once flowed. Once the hole is made it grows, and finally the stream leaves the old meander high and dry as a "fossil" streambed.

This section of Utah supported an Indian population from about 2,000 years ago until about A.D. 1300, and thousands of ruins stud the mesas and canyons of the district, although few sites lie within the Monument. The people were related to the dwellers of the Mesa Verde, in Colorado.

The Monument averages 1830 m (6,000 feet) elevation above the sea, and it supports a considerable wildlife population. Deer are numerous; bighorns winter in the canyons; an occasional mountain lion, or "cougar," comes through; smaller mammals, including coyotes and bobcats, are common.

Since there are no accommodations between Blanding and the Monument, and it is a number of miles through rugged country, you should have ample food supplies before leaving Blanding. At the Monument is a campground for those with bedding and cooking equipment. A park ranger is on duty all year, and it is his pleasure and duty to protect the area and help you to understand and enjoy it. Administration is by the superintendent of Canyonlands National Park, 446 South Main, Moab, Utah 84532.

Navajo

ARIZONA

The Anasazi, (Navajo for "ancient ones") were Indians who occupied the San Juan basin long before the Navajos came. These early people roamed this high plateau country, hunting, trapping, gathering nuts and seeds, and around 800 to 1000 years ago began growing corn and squash on a small scale. As farming gained importance in their economy with its more dependable food supplies, they settled in small villages along edges of flat open valleys, beside streams, near meadows on timbered mesas, and in caves.

The villagers began, in the 12th and 13th centuries, combining into a few larger towns, as in sunny alcoves along Tsegi Canyon. Here they lived until about A.D. 1300, reaching culmination of Anasazi culture in this area. Apparently they left because a long drought and attendant arroyo encroachments severely reduced harvests and destroyed farm land.

Navajo National Monument, established in 1909, embracing 146 hectares (360 acres) and completely surrounded by Navajo Indian Reservation, contains three great cliff dwellings: Betatakin, with possibly 150 rooms; Keet Seel, largest and best preserved in Arizona; and Inscription House, with over 65 rooms. These Kayenta Anasazi probably moved south to the Hopi mesas. The Navajos, who now occupy the district, have been here little more than 100 years.

The Monument is accessible by paved road to Headquarters, near Betatakin, elevation 2,227 m (7,300 feet), and is open year round, 24 hours a day. The visitor center is staffed daily 8 to 5 p.m. (to 6 in summer) and there are campground evening programs in summer. During winter snowstorms the entrance road closes, but the campground remains open. Inscription House, dangerous until stabilized, is not open for visitation.

The Headquarters museum presents the story of the Anasazi and their homes, and here begins the self guiding Sandal Trail, leading to an overlook where you see Betatakin nestled under a huge cliff overhang. Visits to Keet Seel are by reservation only, with tours into the dwelling by rangers at the site. Accessible on horseback by a 26 km (16 mile) round trip trail, the trip

requires a full day, and only experienced hikers should walk it. Arrangements for horses should be made at least a day in advance, at the visitor center or in writing.

Guided walking tours to Betatakin start daily in summer at 8:30 and 1:30 (Daylight Savings Time), and require about 3 hours, mainly because of the steep mile-long climb of 214 m (700 feet) from canyon floor to rim.

The campground, near Headquarters, has tables, fireplaces and water available nearby. Limited camp supplies, mostly canned goods, are available at trading posts: Black Mesa 14 km (9 miles) away, and Kayenta, 51 km (32 miles). Lodging and meals are available at Kayenta, Tuba City, or Tsegi, all between 24 and 105 km (15 and 65 miles). For information and reservations you can write Holiday Inn or Wetherill Inn Motel, Kayenta; Van's Trading Post, Tuba City; or Tsegi Trading Post, Tsegi, Arizona. During summer it is best to have reservations.

Because of difficulty in following some unmarked trails and need to protect ruins as well as visitors, you may not enter any of the Monument's ruins without a guide. Inquiries may be addressed to: Superintendent, Navajo National Monument, Tonalea, Arizona 86044.

Organ Pipe Cactus
ARIZONA

This National Monument was established in 1937 to preserve over 1300 sq km (500 square miles) of superlative Sonoran Desert scenery found just north of the Mexican border. It features rocky canyons, stark mountains, sweeping bajadas and a pleasant winter climate. This vast natural desert garden is populated with a surprisingly varied array of birds and other animals which are adapted to climatic extremes of heat and aridity, and attracted ancestors of the Papago Indians at certain seasons as they harvested wild plant foods to supplement their agricultural crops.

Visitors should stop at the visitor center, 27 km (17 miles) south of the Monument entrance, to study exhibits about desert life; obtain information from park rangers about how best to see the area without harming it or themselves; and in winter to learn about naturalist walks and evening talks. There are two graded scenic loop drives into more interesting and remote portions, and for each there is a self-guiding information leaflet.

The 34 km (21 mile) Ajo Mountain Drive takes you through a series of outstanding desert views, including fine stands of organpipe cactus and teddybear cholla. A steep foot trail to Bull Pasture begins at the Estes Canyon picnic area. This vigorous climb, a mile and a half long, leads to a high and outstandingly scenic area.

The Puerto Blanco Drive, 82 km (51 miles) long, circles the mountain range of the same name and skirts the Mexican border for several miles. At least half a day is required for this trip. Short side roads lead to a manmade oasis and bird paradise at Quitobaquito, and a display of senita cactus in Senita Basin.

Cross-country hiking is possible almost anywhere in the Monument, but climbs or long hikes should not be attempted without first consulting a park ranger. You should check back with him when you return. Desert heat and uncertain water holes are grave dangers to the hiker who is not prepared for them. Summer temperatures in the lower levels of the Monument, 335 to 366 m (1,100 to 1,200 feet) above sea level, frequently range between 38 and 44 C (100 and 110 degrees) in the shade.

No food or lodging is available in the Monument. Motels, restaurants and trailer parks are located in the towns of Ajo, Lukeville, Why and Sonoyta, Mexico. A grocery store, post office, bar, laundromat, motel, curio shop, service station and campgrounds are also located at Lukeville, 8 km (5 miles) south of the visitor center. Limited supplies and gasoline are available in Sonoyta, 3.2 km (2 miles) south of the border.

There is a large campground 2.5 km (1½ miles) south of the visitor center. Back country camping may be done by **permit** only, and drivers of motor vehicles should remember that one set of fresh tire tracks in unspoiled natural desert may remain as a scar for many years in this arid climate.

For additional information, write to the superintendent, Organ Pipe Cactus National Monument, Box 38, Ajo, Arizona 85321.

Padre Island

TEXAS

Padre Island National Seashore is the largest of several such areas in our nation. It occupies the central 129 km (80.5 miles) of the 182 km (113 mile) long Padre Island, stretching along the Texas gulf coast south of Corpus Christi. The island varies in width from a few hundred meters to 5 km (3 miles), and is separated from the mainland by the shallow Laguna Madre, with a maximum width of 16 km (10 miles).

This uninhabited seashore coastline is the longest undeveloped and uncluttered beach in the contiguous United States! Some private and county development has been done at each end of the island, where causeways connect it with Corpus Christi on the north and Port Isabel on the south. Motels and restaurants are located on both ends of the island and in the nearby towns of Corpus Christi and Port Isabel. A concession at Malaquite Beach, 6 km (four miles) south of the National Seashore's northern boundary, offers light lunches, free showers, locker rooms, gift shop, and rental of beach equipment.

A campground at Malaquite Beach is open to the public. A waste disposal station for trailers, restrooms and water is available. Camping is also permitted on the beach south and north of Malaquite.

Padre Island is a textbook example of a barrier island, built by wave action and crowned by wind-formed sand dunes. On the Gulf side is a wide clean beach of sand; next comes the alinement of dunes, reaching to heights of 12 m (40 feet); then grassy flats; and last, on the lagoon side, a vaguely defined shoreline that seems to merge with the waters.

Shell beaches on the Gulf side attest to the abundance of marine snails, clams, and other mollusks. This coast is a very important wintering area for waterfowl. Resident birds include pelicans, egrets, herons, gulls, and terns. An occasional visitor is the seldom seen, but never forgotten, magnificent frigatebird. Among common mammals are jackrabbits, coyotes, and spotted ground squirrels. Woody vegetation is limited to a few groves of scrub live oak in the northern part, but other interesting plants include the partridge pea, croton, beach evening primrose, and morning-glory.

This is a place to sense the inspiring solitude of beach and sea, to watch and hear wild creatures, to loaf, and, for the energetic, to swim and fish. Surf fishing yields redfish, sea trout, black drum, and other species; guides and boats are available in nearby coastal towns for those wishing to catch tarpon, mackerel, sailfish, and snapper.

The climate invites year-round recreation, with cool gulf breezes in summer and warm sunshine in winter. "Northers" sometimes chill the coast, but are usually shortlived. Average January temperature is 14° C (57°); average July temperature is 28° C (83°). Orange and grapefruit groves of the Lower Rio Grande Valley are but a short distance from the southern end of the island.

Interpretive programs in the summer include guided walks on beaches, and through grasslands, and evening programs.

Roads extend 6 km (four miles) into the north end of the National Seashore, with several access roads leading to the beach. Standard vehicles may drive a few miles on the hard packed beach sands at the north end, but four-wheel drive vehicles must be used on most of the beaches. Driving is prohibited on vegetation or on the coastal dunes. For further information write to the superintendent, Padre Island National Seashore, 9405 South Padre Island Drive, Corpus Christi, Texas 78418.

Pecos

NEW MEXICO

Pecos National Monument, containing 138 ha (341 acres) located on the eastern edge of Pueblo country was authorized in 1965. It preserves the structural remains of two villages and a large mission, all of which played a role in the story of Plains-Pueblo contacts.

Forked Lightning Ruin, the earliest of the two villages and inhabited during the 1200's, exhibits material traded from the plains. By 1300, however, this site and others in the near vicinity were abandoned, and many of the people seem to have concentrated into one large pueblo today known as Pecos. This new pueblo, quadrangular in plan and multi-storied, was defensive in all respects with guard houses at each entrance, staggered entrance passageways, and no exterior doorways, all suggesting that enemy pressures, probably nomads on the plains, forced the scattered villagers to consolidate their strength into one pueblo.

The people of Pecos and other pueblos to the west defended themselves against the marauding Apaches and Teyas of the plains until shortly before the entry of the Spaniards in 1540, by which time these plains Indians were friendly with Pecos. Because of its location, this large pueblo became the gateway to the plains for the Spanish exploratory expeditions of the late 1500's. After the 1598 Spanish settlement of New Mexico and after the establishment of missions in the pueblos in the early 1600's, missionaries of the middle 1600's used Pecos as their point of departure in an effort to convert plains groups as far east as central Oklahoma. At the same time, Spaniards also carried on trade with Plains Indians using Pecos as a frontier trading post.

Deeply involved in a rebellion against the Spaniards between 1680 and 1692, Pecos in the early 1700's shifted its attention toward a new threat from the plains, the Comanches sweeping down from the north. By the middle of the century, French traders occasionally broke through the Comanche barrier in an effort to open up traffic with the Southwest, mainly using Pecos as their point of entry. Similarly, when traders from the United States opened up the Santa Fe Trail in the 1820's, the road led to Pecos on the western edge of the plains.

Continued depredations and devastating epidemics of the 1700's and early 1800's played havoc with the people of Pecos, and in 1838 the few surviving families left their homes and joined their linguistic relatives at Jemez. It is a fitting tribute to these people of Pecos that the first major excavations in Southwestern historical archeology were undertaken at this pueblo by Dr. Alfred V. Kidder between 1915 and 1929. His pioneering and definitive work and meetings held on the site led to the foundation of a systematic approach to Southwestern archeology.

Easily accessible from Santa Fe, the Monument lies a few miles off interstate 25 and alternate 84–85. Facilities for visitors presently are being developed for day use only. For further information, write the superintendent, Drawer 11, Pecos, New Mexico 87552.

Petrified Forest

ARIZONA

The most wondrous known display of petrified wood, and part of northeastern Arizona's highly colored Painted Desert, lie within the 382 sq km (147 square miles) of Petrified Forest National Park, established as a National Monument in 1906, and as a National Park in 1962.

Most of the trees did not petrify in place, but were transported millions of years ago by flooding streams and deposited in bays or on sandbars, where rapid burial by mud and sand prevented their decay. The mud and sand, rich in silica-containing volcanic ash, finally hardened into the shales and sandstones of the Chinle Formation. These deposits were buried under at least 915 m (3,000 feet) of sand and silt laid down by shallow seas. Ground water picked up the silica and deposited it in cell tissues of buried trees. The mineral filled the wood solidly, forming petrified logs, in which varying amounts of original organic matter remain. The mottled color patterns were caused by various minerals, including copper, iron and manganese.

After the trees were buried, the region slowly rose, to become arid and desert-like, while weather action wore it down. Stream erosion eventually exposed some of the petrified logs, and has shaped the Painted Desert badlands.

The earth surface here consists of water-deposited layers of volcanic ash, interbedded with thin layers of shale, sandstone, and river gravel. Alteration of the ash has converted it into claylike bentonite, hard and strong when dry, soupy when wet, and thus easily weathered into ravines, conical hills, and ridges.

Park elevation ranges from 1616 to 1891 m (5,300 to 6,200 feet), and today it receives only 25 cm (10 inches) of annual precipitation. Most of the plants are small and inconspicuous, adapted to the way of life permitted by a rather rugged climate of drought, summer heat, and winter cold. Showier blossoms of yuccas, mariposas and cactuses bloom only in spring, but aster, painted cup, rabbitbrush and sunflowers bloom through much of the summer.

Bird species include horned larks, house finches, rock wrens, phoebes, and several sparrows. Over a dozen species of snakes and lizards occur, including the prairie rattlesnake. Mammals include black-tail jackrabbit, cottontail, white-tail antelope squirrel, skunk, coyote, bobcat, porcupine, and pronghorn.

Refreshments, lunches, and gasoline can be purchased at Painted Desert Oasis and Rainbow Forest Lodge, establishments 42 km (26 miles) apart near the two entrances. At Rainbow Forest and Painted Desert are small picnic sites with tables. There are no overnight facilities. Backpack camping only, in wilderness areas, is by permit. Nearest public campgrounds are in national forests nearly 160 km (100 miles) away. Motels and restaurants are located along the highways and in nearby communities.

You should stop at Painted Desert visitor center and Administration Building for information about this and other units of the National Park System in the Southwest. Exhibits at Rainbow Forest Museum explain the Park's natural history. Wayside exhibits at major interest points along the park road, from Painted Desert to Rainbow Forest, will increase your enjoyment and understanding.

Inquiries should be addressed to the superintendent, Petrified Forest National Park, Arizona 86028.

Pipe Spring
ARIZONA

Gunlock Bill (William) Hamblin was considered one of the best rifle shots in the Southwest a little over a century ago. His skill was put to the test one day in 1858, by other members of the Jacob Hamblin camping party. They had been sent out by Brigham Young, to explore and report on the Colorado River country, to learn more of the Hopis, and if possible convert them to the Mormon faith.

The group was camped only 16 km (10 miles) south of the present Utah border and well to the north of the Colorado, in what we now call the Arizona Strip. A member of the group tricked Hamblin into trying to shoot through a silk handkerchief at 50 paces. With the softly yielding handkerchief, suspended only by the top edge, the bullet didn't go through the silk but merely pushed it aside. Mildly aggravated, Hamblin dared one of the men to set his pipe faced toward them. He wagered he could shoot the bottom out without touching the rim. The bet was accepted, Hamblin performed the feat, and the spring got it's name!

Pioneer cattleman James M. Whitmore, built a dugout in 1863 at Pipe Spring using it as a headquarters for his cattle and sheep operation. He and his herder were killed by raiding Navajos in January of 1866. The Mormon Church acquired the property from Whitmore's widow in 1870. That same year Bishop A. P. Winsor arrived with his family to care for the property and to start a tithing herd for the Mormon Church. By late 1871 "Winsor Castle", a fort-like structure, was completed under the direction of Joseph W. Young. Near the base of the colorful Vermillion Cliffs, it consisted of two 2-story red sandstone buildings facing each other across a courtyard closed at the ends with high sandstone walls and heavy gates. There were defensive loop holes in the walls, and a firing platform several feet below the top of one wall. One building was built directly over the spring and water flowed from it through the other building. This afforded a protected water source.

Pipe Spring operated as a church tithing ranch for several decades before passing into private hands around 1895. It had several successive owners until Charles Heaton arranged with Stephen Mather to hand it over to the National Park Service. The 16 ha (40-acre) National Monument was proclaimed in 1923, to commemorate the courage, foresight, and faith of the pioneers in general, the Mormons in particular. Today the buildings stand as they did in the 1870's, and contain a fine collection of period furniture, blacksmith and carpenter tools, and farm implements.

From April through September a Living History Program is conducted. Demonstrations of various activities from pioneer life of a hundred years ago include cattle branding, farming with a team and plow, cooking and baking on an old wood stove, cheese making, butter churning, quilting, spinning, and weaving.

Pipe Spring is about 1525 m (5,000 feet) above sea level and experiences warm summer days with cool evenings. The region is sparsely vegetated with pinyons, junipers, sage, and rabbitbrush. Many small cacti and desert flowers bloom in May and early June. Trees planted by the pioneers to make Pipe Spring a true oasis include silverleaf cottonwoods, Lombardy poplars and Pottawattamie plum trees. Wildlife includes jackrabbits, desert cottontails, gophers, squirrels, coyotes, badgers, and porcupine. Birds and lizards are abundant.

Daily guide service is offered through the historic buildings and grounds. While there are no camping or picnicking facilities in the Monument, there is a picnic area nearby on the Kaibab Paiute Reservation, and 48 campsites with complete hookups, plus an area for primitive camping. Inquiries may be addressed to: superintendent, Pipe Spring National Monument, Moccasin, Arizona, 86022.

Rainbow Bridge

UTAH

Rainbow Bridge lies in rugged sandstone canyon country just south of the Colorado River, in extreme southern Utah. Although of natural origin, its astounding symmetry and size qualify it as a wonder of the world.

Many millions of years ago sluggish streams here flowed southwest across a broad flood plain, depositing mud and sand which later consolidated into reddish-browns to purples of the Kayenta Formation, the upper part of which is exposed beneath Rainbow Bridge.

During a gradual change to desert conditions, westerly winds brought quantities of sand, depositing it in large, sweeping dunes. This sand, now weakly cemented, is the cliff-forming, pale-orange to pale reddish-brown Navajo Sandstone, in which the Rainbow Bridge and Bridge Canyon were formed.

For nearly 100 million years the region alternated as desert, flood plain, swamp, or was partly covered by lakes or shallow marine waters, which buried the Navajo Sandstone at least 1525 m (5,000 feet) deep. Then, 60 million years or more ago, began a slow, general uplift of the Colorado Plateau. In places, as at Navajo Mountain, this was exaggerated as masses of molten rock moved upward, forcing overlying rock to dome above them.

The present scene resulted from stream erosion, partly by the Colorado and its tributaries, cutting thousands of feet into ancient rock layers now high above sea level. Early stream-cutting was slow, and courses meandered widely; with more uplift and land tilting, streams acquired greater force and sped their downcutting in those old meanders.

Rainbow Bridge formed during entrenchment of Bridge Creek, flowing from Navajo Mountain northwest to the Colorado (Lake Powell), and its canyon was carved through Navajo Sandstone into the upper Kayenta Formation. At the harder Kayenta Rock, downcutting was more difficult, and the stream path widened, undercutting canyon walls until it cut through the base of a meander loop's thin spur. The stream widened its new course to form a sandstone bridge.

Predominant color of the great arch is salmon-pink, with dark streaks. As rain fell on the upper part, hematite in the sandstone washed down the sides and was deposited by evaporation, leaving the variegated reds and browns. Under late afternoon sun the brilliant color possibly accounted for the Indian legend that the arch is a rainbow turned to stone.

Rainbow Bridge Canyon has springs, where water, seeping down through Navajo Sandstone to the harder Kayenta Formation, emerged. Lush plant growth occurs at these protected poolsides, including maidenhair fern and wild orchids. Lovely redbud blooms along the stream in April. On drier slopes are painted cups, lupines, daisies, asters, evening-primrose, sego-lily and yucca.

Probably the first white man to see Rainbow Bridge was some wandering prospector. No accurate publicity appeared until the 1909 discovery by Dr. Byron Cummings and W. B. Douglass. The National Monument, containing 65 ha (160 acres), was established the next year.

There are no accommodations or facilities at the Bridge, but a marina is located 1.6 km (a mile) away on Lake Powell and provides gasoline, water, and camping provisions. You should pack out tin cans and other refuse when leaving. The nearest town with hospital, markets, motels and restaurants, is Page. The superintendent of Glen Canyon National Recreation Area, Box 1507, Page, Arizona 86040, is in charge of the Monument.

Rocky Mountain

COLORADO

The dazzling magnificence of Rocky Mountain National Park is fitting for a "top of the nation" position astride the continental divide. Here more than 71 peaks rise over 3660 m (12,000 feet) above sea level to puncture the blue of the sky, reflected in scores of crystalline lakes.

The park embraces 1071 sq km (412 square miles) of the Rockies' Front Range, north and west of Denver, Colorado, extending on the north to within 48 km (30 miles) of the Wyoming border. Established by Act of Congress in 1915, it adjoins Shadow Mountain National Recreation Area on its southwest flank.

To most of us, tundra, glacier, moraine and cirque are names only, vague memories from school text books. Here they "come alive" as you travel from deep valleys to above treeline and find condensed within a few miles a cross sectional view of what titanic earth building forces accomplished. The ancestral Rocky Mountains began about 300 million years ago with uplift of a sea area. Cycles of invasion by seas and renewed uplift followed. During the last 70 million years came periods of uplift, vulcanism and erosion. During the great Ice Age the continental ice cap formed to the north, while separate local glaciers, of more recent origin, developed and flourished here. Small remnants of these exist in the Park today, although on a "bare subsistence level."

The National Park Service offers excellent summer opportunity for becoming acquainted with the park, through guided walks, campfire programs and other activities. You can drive the 80 km (50 miles) of Trail Ridge Road from Estes Park on the east to Grand Lake on the west, and see the above-treeline "roof of the world," in a three or four hour trip. There are other road tours, plus trails for hiking and mountain climbing. Fishing may be enjoyed (with Colorado license). Concessioners provide horseback riding. You may wish to stay in one of the park's campgrounds, or you may come in winter to enjoy winter activities.

While the geologist thrills over text-book display on physiographic features here, and the camera fan finds it a dream world for photographers, nature lovers can revel in the abundance of plant and animal life. Occasionally seen are elk, bighorn, and mule deer. Beaver are common and coyote music is heard on autumn and winter evenings. Marmots and pikas are a part of the high country scene. More than 150 species of birds are regularly seen. No wildlife may be fed or molested.

The park is big, beautiful and rugged, therefore it can be dangerous. Storms arise quickly, and are sometimes severe. Visitors should not over estimate their strength and endurance on high altitude hikes. Those with any kind of a heart condition should monitor their mountain activities closely. Hikers should never climb alone, and children should not run downhill. All visitors should be careful to check with information stations and visitor centers for information and safety advice on roads and trails. The high altitude and varying climatic conditions dictate different opening and closing dates for different districts. The Park and the adjoining Shadow Mountain National Recreation Area are administered by a superintendent, whose address is Estes Park, Colorado 80517.

Saguaro

ARIZONA

The huge saguaro cactus grows only in the Sonoran Desert, a choice part of which is preserved in the 320 sq km (123 square-mile) Saguaro National Monument, in two separated areas.

The older east side, 26 km (16 miles) east of Tucson, Arizona was established in 1933. It contains an altitudinal range from 824 m (2,700 feet) above sea level in the Cactus Forest to 2643 m (8,666 feet) atop Mica Mountain in the Rincons. An average rainfall of 30 cm (12 inches) in the Cactus Forest increases to 75 cm (30 inches) per year on the mountain top, and the average July high of 34C. (94 degrees F.) in the Cactus Forest drops to 20C. (68 F.) at 2440 m (8,000 feet)! Plant growth and animal forms range from desert types of Mexico to forest species similar to those of Southern Canada.

Exhibits at the visitor center explain the location and occurrence of world and regional deserts, and how living things adapt to the arid environment. Here you may sit in comfortable chairs to watch, through ceiling-high windows, desert creatures as they come to a waterhole to drink during the dry seasons. After thus "getting acquainted" you likely will drive the 14 km (9-mile) loop road through aging giants of the Cactus Forest, to park at pullouts and follow short marked trails where you can get to know desert plants by sight and by smell.

A varied array of mammal, reptile and bird species cope with the heat, drought, and wide day-to-night temperature range. Peccaries and mule deer are at home here. Other inhabitants include coyotes, bobcats, cottontails and jackrabbits, and occasional skunks, gray foxes, and badgers. The desert tortoise and Gila mon-ster live here, and some snakes, including an occasional western diamondback rattlesnake or a rare Sonoran coral snake. The cactus wren, curve-billed thrasher, Gila woodpecker and Gambel's quail all are part of the picture.

There are over 105 km (65 miles) of maintained trails. If you are the rugged, well-conditioned hiker and wish to climb on the mountain trails, be sure to obtain a Back Country use permit at the visitor center.

You may also wish to visit the Tucson Mountain Unit which is 26 km (16 miles) west of Tucson. It was added to the Monument in 1961. En route is the Arizona-Sonora Desert Museum, an outstanding presentation of Sonoran Desert natural history, and well worth a visit.

In the Tucson Mountain unit, contrasting with the slowly dying Cactus Forest of the Rincon Mountain section, is an immensely vigorous growth of a younger saguaro population. These contrasts emphasize how thin is the margin between life and death in this hostile environment. The success of numerous plant species in making a rich vegetative cover for much of this arid land makes it look utterly unlike the deserts of our imagination.

Roads here are still graded dirt (1977), but picnic areas with tables, shelters, and restrooms are available. Water is available at the visitor center at both sections, but not available in the picnic areas. There are self-guiding nature trails, and a self-guiding auto tour.

Neither of the two sections of the Monument has facilities for camping, lodging, food, or gasoline.

For information, write the superintendent, P.O. Box 17210, Tucson, Arizona 85731.

Sunset Crater

ARIZONA

Sunset Crater National Monument, containing 11.7 sq km (4½ square miles), was established in 1930 to preserve a colorful volcanic cinder cone. The eruption of this youngest member in the 7800 sq km (3,000 square mile) San Francisco Mountains volcanic field, was a minor event, geologically speaking, but drastically altered the lives of Indian farmers and hunters living in the area. Not only were local people affected, but those who lived at Walnut Canyon to the south, and Wupatki, to the north.

Sometime between A.D. 1064 and A.D. 1250, the few Indians, referred to as the Sinagua, living in and near the area were startled by a series of volcanic events. The earth trembled and roared with the explosive violence which sent fiery globs of molten lava, cinders, and ash into the sky. Wind carried away the lighter materials, while heavy objects fell around the vent to make the mass of smoking black rocks and cinders grow higher.

The great, black mound grew rapidly as each of several eruptions occurred. Molten lava, a liquid river of fire, broke out at the base of the growing cinder cone, and in its advance buried hastily abandoned corn fields and pithouses.

When the eruptions were over, there remained the 305 m (1000 foot) high cinder cone. Slowly cooling flows of jagged lava lay at its base, and black volcanic ash covered hundreds of square miles. Hot springs and vapors seeped out from cracks around the crater's vent depositing minerals around the rim and staining the cinders red and yellow. Today, the summit seems to glow with hues of a perpetual sunset.

During these violent eruptions a redistribution of prehistoric Indian populations took place. Some Indians in the pre-eruptive period already knew the value of volcanic cinders as moisture-retaining mulch, from having farmed around the edges of older cinder fields. Others quickly discovered greatly increased crop yields when they planted in the ash of Sunset Crater. They moved to the area where most ash fell — a previously barren land now known as the Wupatki Basin.

Their relatively brief but intense period of occupation produced the many structures (now in ruins) of Wupatki National Monument, 29 km (18 miles) by paved road to the northeast.

The Sunset Crater visitor center, located 3 km (2 miles) from Highway 89, is at an elevation of 2135 m (7,000 feet) and open all year, although the road may be closed temporarily by heavy winter snow storms. A modern campground is located across from the National Park Service visitor center. There are also picnic facilities in the area.

At the base of the crater is the Lava Flow Nature Trail, which introduces visitors to most of the geologic features associated with a volcano. Here are found the ice cave, fumaroles, squeeze-ups, and, of course, the impressive lava flow. To the east is located the Painted Desert; to the west are the San Francisco Peaks containing Humphreys Peak, 3864 m (12,670 feet), the highest point in Arizona.

For more information write to the superintendent, Sunset Crater National Monument, Tuba Star Route, Flagstaff, Arizona 86001.

Timpanogos Cave
UTAH

In the beautiful Wasatch Mountains of north-central Utah, a few miles southeast of Salt Lake City, is mighty Mount Timpanogos. Its snow-crowned head reaches 3584 m (11,750 feet) above sea level, towering above Utah's Great Basin. On the north slope of this giant is a series of small, jewel-like caverns, renowned for their beauty.

Timpanogos Cave National Monument, set aside by Presidential proclamation in 1922 and placed under care of the Department of Agriculture, came into the National Park System in 1933. It now contains 101 ha (250 acres), and is administered under a super-intendent, whose address is Rt. 2, Box 200, American Fork, Utah 84003. Monument offices are located at the visitor center, elevation 1389 m (5,665 feet).

To reach the cave entrance you follow the 2.4 km (1½ miles) of winding trail from the Monument visitor center up the steep slope of Mount Timpanogos, rising 325 m (1,065 feet) in route. This path offers outstanding scenic views of the Wasatch Mountains, Utah Valley, and American Fork Canyon. Numbered markers along the trail correspond to paragraphs in a self-guiding trail booklet, and give you a "speaking" acquaintance with many of the interesting plants, geologic features and views along the way.

There are three caves, all connected by man made tunnels. Much of the interior is covered with a filigree of rare lemon-yellow, green, buff, pink and white trans-lucent crystals which sparkle like jewels. Helictites and thin stalactites are interwoven and twisted to produce a maze of beauty, and tiny pools of water reflect the scene.

The cave formations are still being deposited. Water which is slightly acidic seeps through the overlying limestone, dissolving tiny amounts of rock and then depositing the minerals in the caves. Countless water droplets hang on the lower tips of the formations. As the water drips, calcite and other minerals remain behind to help develop the spectacular features. Some of the minerals are carried to the floor of the caves, where conditions are suitable for development of other features.

Elevation of the rock strata which produced the Wasatch Range resulted in stresses, causing the rock to break. Along these fractures huge blocks of rock moved past each other, resulting in a fault zone. Along two of the fault zones the caves were formed. Ground water easily passed through these areas of broken and pulverized rock. This water was largely responsible for development of the caves, by solution, abrasion, and erosion. As American Fork Canyon was cut deeper through stream erosion the water table was lowered. At this time the cave environment changed from cavern development and enlargement to cavern decoration, which still continues.

At the visitor center you may learn more of the fascinating story of the caves, through exhibits and an audiovisual program. The caves are normally open from May 1 until November 1. During winter months snow and ice close the cave trail, although the visitor center is open year round.

Tonto

ARIZONA

Central Arizona around Theodore Roosevelt Lake is a rugged region of mountain barriers and deep canyons, and here a group of Pueblo Indians, the Salado, built and occupied the famous Tonto cliff dwellings in the 14th Century. They were somewhat isolated by their surroundings from neighboring people outside the basin area, but in the tremendous altitudinal range of their land, from forested mountain tops to desert canyon bottoms, they had a very wide range of native animal and plant foods available with which to supplement farm crops.

Tonto National Monument, established in 1907, includes in its 454 ha (1,120 acres) two major cliff dwellings, the Upper and Lower Ruins, and several small surface sites. Flood plains of the Salt River, (outside the Monument boundaries) were the croplands of these prehistoric people, and until the valley was flooded by the lake, ancient irrigation canals were still visable 3.2 to 6.4 km (2 to 4 miles) from the Tonto Ruins and 305 m (1,000 feet) lower in elevation.

About A.D. 1000, the first Salado in the Tonto Basin began building small, compact pueblos on the valley floor. Since they depended on the Salt River, they were later named the Salado (spanish for "salty"). Their pottery indicates close connections with other Pueblo Indians, of the Little Colorado River Drainage to the north. By the 1300's, some Salado had built villages in the cliffs and mountains high above the Basin, possibly for reasons of defense, though their enemies remain unknown. Salado abandonment of the area in the 1400's seem to coincide with a general exodus of Puebloan peoples from the southern mountains of the Southwest. Some may have gone northeast to join the Zuni, and others may have been absorbed by tribes to the south and east.

Visitors to Tonto arrive first at the visitor center, which contains specimens of one of the best-preserved collections of prehistoric fabrics and vegetal material in the Southwest. From there a self-guiding trail 800 m (one-half mile) long climbs 107 m (350 feet) to the Lower Ruin. This village of 19 rooms, built in a natural cave at 961 m (3,150 feet) above sea level, has high walls of unshaped quartzite stone laid in mud mortar; even some of the original timbered, mud-covered roofs remain, as well as ancient finger marks in the wall plaster. The Upper Ruin, a larger but more fragile structure of 40 rooms, is situated in a cave in a higher promontory to the south. For safety and protection visitors enter this ruin only with a ranger guide, and by advance arrangement.

Tonto National Monument is open the year round, with most comfortable weather between late October and early June. A superintendent is in charge, whose address is P.O. Box 707, Roosevelt, Arizona 85545.

Tumacacori

ARIZONA

Three centuries ago Spain was a great colonial power in the New World, claiming territory far north of present Mexico. In defense of her far-flung empire she dotted her frontiers with presidios (garrison posts for soldiers) and kept the Spanish flag flying to warn off possible aggressor nations. The scattered soldiers alone could not control thousands of Indians; so shoulder to shoulder with them came missionary priests carrying the Cross of conversion. Priests were responsible for saving and civilizing the Indians in missions, the greatest of Spain's frontier institutions.

The first missionaries in Pimeria Alta (land of the Upper Pimas) were Jesuits, and one of the most intrepid and brilliant of these was Father Kino. In January 1691, he visited one of the mission villages in what is now northern Sonora. Here he met a delegation of Indians from Tumacacori, to the north, who carried crosses with them and asked him to visit their village too. They were interested in the livestock, fruit trees, and wheat that the Father was giving to mission Indians, and they were curious about the new religion.

So Father Kino journeyed to Tumacacori, on the banks of the Santa Cruz River, and there before the assembled Pimas he celebrated Mass. Thus Christianity came to southern Arizona, beginning 150 years of mission history for Tumacacori, first under the Jesuits, and after 1768 under the Franciscans. By the Gadsden Purchase of 1853 that portion of Mexico containing Tumacacori and Tucson became part of the United States. The mission church was by then abandoned and falling into ruins. In 1908 the present church building and 4 ha (10 acres) of land became a National Monument. Today a resident superintendent lives on the grounds; his mailing address is P.O. Box 67, Tumacacori, Arizona 85640.

The present church of Tumacacori dates from the Franciscan period. Built by Indians under direction of a priest, it was started about 1795 and substantially completed by 1822. The massive adobe walls, with their fired-brick bell tower, barrel-vaulted sacristy, and the great dome of the sanctuary still stand. Today's visitor may wander through the mission church, the cemetery and mortuary chapel, the convento ruins, mission storehouse, and the modern Spanish style patio garden and museum building. Visitors enjoy the famous dioramas in the museum, and on the walk through the church and grounds use a trail guide booklet, cued to different trail-side exhibits. The Monument is open daily, from 8:30 to 5:30.

There are no campgrounds or other visitor facilities, but a good highway leads to Tucson 76 km (47 miles) north, and to the border city of Nogales 29 km (18 miles) south.

Tuzigoot

ARIZONA

A feudal baron of long ago would have enjoyed Tuzigoot (Two-ZEE-GOOT) Hill, in central Arizona, for his seat of operations. Here a long, limestone ridge rose 37 m (120 feet) above fertile river terraces, to provide a commanding view over many acres of superb farmland in a great ox-bow curve. Here the Verde River had cut through a ridge to desert an old meander route around the tip of this hill. Modern Peck's Lake occupies part of the old meander.

Atop the hill, prehistoric Pueblo Indian architecture graphically demonstrates population trends in the Verde Valley during the 12th, 13th and 14th centuries. Early in its history, about A.D. 1150, Tuzigoot was a small 12-room pueblo on the ridge, typical of many comparable ones in the Verde Valley. In the early 1200's numerous dry-farming villages in the valley were abandoned in favor of sites close to streams, such as Tuzigoot, where irrigation was possible.

Apparently these dry-farmers gone "wet," and drifting "into town" as it were, gave Tuzigoot a modest building boom, resulting in an expansion down the south slope of the ridge.

Toward the end of the 1200's Tuzigoot experienced its greatest and final growth with an influx of related peoples from the plateau area to the north. By now limited stream terrace farmlands were overtaxed in the valley, and the hospitality of these peaceful folk seems to have been tempered by expediency; to protect stored foods against raids by hungry neighbors it became necessary to discontinue exterior doors on the pueblo.

At its peak, Tuzigoot was two stories high, with 89 ground-floor and probably 21 second-floor rooms, cov-ering an area 31 m (100 feet) wide by 153 m (500 feet) long. Rooms were large, averaging 3.6 × 5.4 m (12 × 18 feet). Residents entered by ladders to the roof-tops, then through ceiling hatchways into rooms.

Reasons for abandonment of Tuzigoot and numer-ous sister towns in the Verde Valley, probably during the 1400's, are not entirely clear. It is possible that population pressures, over-use of available farmland, and epidemics in crowded pueblos could have pro-duced such intolerable situations that gradual migration outward was desirable. (The white man is not the first, or only, human group, to exhaust natural resources!) Hopi and Zuni Indians of today have traditions sug-gesting that some of their ancestors came from the Verde Valley.

When Antonio Espejo and his Spanish soldiers en-tered the valley in 1583, they found Yavapai Indians living in thatched huts; the pueblos were all long-abandoned and in ruins.

To establish a much needed WPA project for un-employed smelter workers, United Verde Copper Company deeded 17 ha (43 acres) to the Verde School District. University of Arizona archeologists Louis R. Caywood and Edward H. Spicer excavated the site in 1933–34. The school district donated the ruins and its collection to the National Park Service in 1939.

The area is open year-round. Elevation is between 1007 and 1068 m (3,300 and 3,500 feet) above sea level, with warm-temperature climate. The ruins and self-guiding trail are open daily, as is the museum-visitor center. The superintendent in charge has the mailing address of P.O. Box 68, Clarkdale, Arizona 86324.

Walnut Canyon

ARIZONA

Walnut Canyon National Monument, located in northern Arizona, preserves more than 100 cliff dwellings in a beautiful canyon setting. These dwellings are examples of the Sinagua culture, a local development of the Pueblo agricultural peoples of the Southwest. Although known to wandering hunters of 3,000 years ago, the major occupation began here after the mid-1000's, following the eruption of Sunset Crater, and continued through the mid-1200's.

In addition to cliff dwellings there are also numerous surface structures on the rim. The water supply was a stream 122 m (400 feet) below the rim, but the agricultural fields on the plateau above were dependent on natural rainfall, partly controlled by check dams.

The environment is that of the pinyon-juniper zone of approximately 2135 m (7,000 feet) elevation, but due to varying exposure of sunlight on the steep canyon walls, there is a mixture of vegetation varying from Douglas-fir to yucca and prickly pear cactus. The Arizona black walnut gives the canyon its name. These plants were very important in the daily life of the Sinagua.

Walnut Canyon is over 32 km (20 miles) long. The monument lies at its midpoint which is the deepest part of the canyon. It cuts through the Kaibab limestone and Coconino sandstone plateau, and the weaker limestone areas which were eroded away provide the ledges in which the dwellings were built. Side canyons and smaller drainages provided steep but easy access to the stream. The creek bed is now dry because of a dam at its headwaters which forms Flagstaff's main water supply.

Life here was good. There was water, farmland, a variety of plants and animals to supplement the diet and provide important tools, and natural shelter in the canyon ledges. Peak population was perhaps 500 and there was a good deal of trade with other peoples of different cultures. Why this way of life in the canyon ended is not known, but there are several clues. There was a drought in the 1200's which may have forced abandonment into better-watered irrigation lands in the Verde Valley. The land may have been worn out or there may have been disease. Life was peaceful and there is no evidence of warfare or raiding by other people. It was probably a slow gradual abandonment for a variety of reasons, capped by a decrease in usable rainfall. Their descendants may be among the present-day Hopi and Zuni.

A paved 1.2 km (¾ mile) round trip self-guiding trail leads into the canyon and circles 25 of the best preserved cliff dwelling rooms. The trail is steep, 56 m (185 feet) of steps, which makes a fairly strenuous but not difficult walk. A level trail along the rim gives overlook views of the canyon ruins, and also goes near two ruins built near the rim farming fields. It is 1 km (⅝ of a mile) long.

There is an exhibit room, picnic area, and several viewpoints of the canyon and cliff dwellings. A superintendent, whose address is Route 1, Box 25, Flagstaff, Arizona 86001, is in charge. The monument is open year around, and reached by a 4.8 km (3 mile) road off U.S. 66 (Interstate 40). There is a small entrance fee.

White Sands

NEW MEXICO

The Tularosa Basin of south-central New Mexico lies between two north-south mountain ranges, and contains the world's largest gypsum desert. White Sands National Monument, established in 1933, includes nearly 598 sq km (230 square miles) of the basin.

White Sands has three great values: wilderness, scientific, and recreational. You may step from your car in the 26 km (16 mile) loop drive in the heart of the dunes and hike over a mound into a world untouched by man. The blue sky overhead rests on an immensity of rolling white hills flowing in all directions. In the distance are the dark purple walls of the San Andres Mountains on the west and the Sacramento Mountains on the east. You are 1,220 m (4,000 feet) above sea level, and the largest dunes are over 12 m (40 feet) high.

Gypsum, dissolved by seasonal rain and melting snow in the surrounding mountains, has been carried down for thousands of years into intermittent Lake Lucero, the lowest part of this basin with no surface outlet. Here in the western part of the Monument, sun and wind evaporate the water, leaving a gypsum-crystal encrusted dry lake bed. Arid southwest winds persistently scour the area and the alkali flats to the north. Weathering breaks down the gypsum crystals into white grains of sand, swept northeastward by wind and piled into dunes, which creep forward 9 m (30 feet) or more a year near Lake Lucero and less than 30 cm (one foot) a year in the leading edge where dunes are almost stabilized by plant growth.

The loose sand is only inches deep, for at greater depths the gypsum is partially solidified by crystal growth between grains. In low areas between dunes water is a few feet down, and moisture only a few inches. Here grow species of rugged plants able to withstand alkaline water. Larger plants occasionally live in the dunes, growing roots 12 m (40 feet) to reach water and hold their sandy base from shifting faster than they grow.

At the Monument visitor center, 24 km (15 miles) southwest of Alamogordo are museum exhibits explaining the geology and natural history of the dunes, and revealing some interesting adaptations of wild creatures to the exacting and unusual sands environment. Here publications about the area may be purchased, and a concessioner offers souvenirs and refreshments. The scenic dunes drive is open year round, with the visitor center closed only on Christmas Day.

Naturalist conducted activities include evening programs and nature walks during summer months. Special full-moon night programs highlight summer interpretive activities. Monthly motor tours to Lake Lucero, usually dry, are also available.

Once past the visitor center and into the sands, rare is the person, young or old, who can resist the alluring beauty of the dunes.

When in the monument vicinity, tune your radio to 1610 AM for latest information. A superintendent is in charge of the area. His address is Box 458, Alamogordo, New Mexico 88310.

Wupatki

ARIZONA

Imagine yourself in north-central Arizona, 1400 years ago. Here the San Francisco Mountains dominate the scene, and with the surrounding volcanic field cover about 7800 sq km (3,000 square miles). The area is studded with volcanic peaks, cinder cones, and lava flows created in the last two million years.

A few Indian farmers, referred to as the Sinagua, are living in the arid sandstone country north-east of the peaks. Their homes are pithouses, which effectively keep out the summer heat and winter cold. They lead a meagre existence at best, for only the very best areas have enough moisture for growing crops. Such areas are the locations of natural springs, meadows, and the soil around old cinder cones.

Several centuries later, with little change in the landscape or the people, there occurred a series of momentous events, beginning in the 11th century. The latest eruptions of the great volcanic field came with a roaring and trembling in the earth, as Sunset Crater had its fiery birth, building a high cone and spewing forth fine, black volcanic cinders and ash to blanket the land for many miles around.

This brief desolation of the countryside frightened the people badly, but it wasn't long before they began ''cashing in'' on the superb, moisture-conserving mulch, which enriched the land and enabled crops to be grown much more successfully. Prior to the eruption, the Sinagua sites were located near old cinder cones close to the San Francisco Peaks where they farmed in the old ash fall areas. A changed environment made farming possible in previously arid lands and settlement of the area now called Wupatki began. These prehistoric settlers not only farmed, but maintained extensive trade routes which extended as far as the Pacific.

During the relatively brief occupation of the late 11th, the 12th, and early 13th centuries, more than 800 Indian structures were built in the 143 sq km (55-square mile) area which now makes up Wupatki National Monument.

One of the most important pueblos built here was Wupatki itself, which contained over 100 rooms and stood three stories high. Others included Citadel, Lomaki, and Wukoki, all beautifully made of dressed sandstone slabs in graded courses. Near the town of Wupatki was an open-air amphitheater, possibly used for public ceremonies, and below lay a ceremonial ball court, also of stone masonry, possibly introduced by the migrants from central Arizona, to the south.

During the early 1200's people began leaving the area. Winds stripped the soil of its protective ash, and in A.D. 1215 a severe and devastating drowth began. By 1225 Wupatki was a ghost town. This was typical of the general exodus during that century to more favored spots.

Today, our time traveler is in his own era, and can visit Wupatki Ruins with self-guiding trail booklet. In the visitor center are attractive and informative exhibits descriptive of the life here long ago. Elevation is 1495 m (4900 feet) above sea level, and the area is open the year round. Paved road leads south 29 km (18 miles) to Sunset Crater National Monument. More information may be obtained by writing to the superintendent, Wupatki-Sunset Crater National Monuments, Tuba Star Route, Flagstaff, Arizona 86001.

Zion

UTAH

Zion Canyon, in southwestern Utah, has been called "the best known example of a deep, narrow, vertically-walled chasm readily accessible for observation." Lavishly colored sheer-wall formations make the area a color photographer's dream. The Park, established as a National Monument in 1909, became Zion National Park in 1919, and today embraces nearly 598 sq km (230 square miles) of deep canyons, sheer rock walls and impressive individual rock masses, combined into a fabulously beautiful region, ideal for "back country" exploring. In few, if any, other places in the U.S. is geological faulting, as a landscape-forming process, so impressively shown.

For best use of your time, go first to the visitor center near the South Entrance for information service and orientation programs, and museum exhibits which interpret natural and human history of the Park. A uniformed employee will gladly help you plan your stay and advise concerning conducted tours, nature hikes, evening illustrated talks, and other scheduled programs.

Park roads are for seeing, not speeding, so the speed limits must be observed; and your lights must be working properly to navigate the 1.6 km (mile-long) tunnel on the Zion-Mount Carmel Highway. Trails are a safety factor in this rugged country, so when you use them, stay on them; and when you attempt more difficult trails check with a park ranger **beforehand,** indicating where you plan to go and when you'll return. Wheelchairs are the only vehicles permitted on trails.

Zion has extensive camping facilities, but even so, they are sometimes full to capacity. Picnicking is limited to specific areas. Overnight accommodations are provided by T.W.A. Services Inc. at its Lodge, and by various motels in Springdale, adjacent to the Park. The Lodge season is usually early June to Labor Day. Facilities in Springdale are available year round.

Mountain climbing and back country exploring in the Kolob section are for those who know what they are about, are in good health, and are not bothered by altitudes ranging from about 1220 m (4,000 feet) to nearly 2440 m (8,000). Hiking and sight seeing opportunities on 249 km (155 miles) of trails are unexcelled. Trails vary to suit every need, with some of the most fascinating ones quite short and easy to travel.

You can take horseback trips with experienced guides. Or you can go on tours of the Park and to other nearby points of interest. These tours are by Color Country Tours, and start on regular schedules in summer from Cedar City, Utah, which is served by bus and airlines. Tours at other seasons are by special arrangement.

The unsurpassed scenery contains impressive variety in plant life, from upper desert forms to lush evergreen forest, and supports a wealth of wildlife.

Zion is a "must" for you to see, but you can't do it well in an hour, or several hours. Plan a longer visit if possible. For more information, write to the superintendent at Springdale, Utah 84767.

How To Get There

The following information, alphabetically by areas, is up-to-date and approved by area superintendents as of late 1977. It lists all National Park Service areas in the Southwest open for public use.

Alibates — Open on limited basis. Access is by the Bates Canyon Information Station off Texas highway 136 at Lake Meredith Recreation Area, northeast of Amarillo.

Amistad — Access to the reservoir area in the U.S. is by paved road from Del Rio, Texas, 19 km (12 miles) west on U.S. 90. Mexico's Highway 57 and other good highways link the interior of Mexico to the border city of Ciudad Acuña, across from Del Rio, Texas.

Arches — Entrance road is 8 km (5 miles) north of Moab, Utah, on U.S. 163. U.S. 163 joins U.S. 50 at Crescent Junction to the north, runs through Durango to the southeast, and can be reached by turning off U.S. 66 at Gallup, New Mexico.

Aztec Ruins — Located about 1.6 km (one mile) northwest of Aztec, New Mexico, and is reached by U.S. Highway 550 or New Mexico Highway 44.

Bandelier — Located 74 km (46 miles) west of Santa Fe, New Mexico, the area is reached from Santa Fe north on U.S. 285 to Pojoaque, then west on New Mexico 4. Approach may also be made through the Jemez Mountains from Albuquerque via Interstate 25 and New Mexico 44 and 4, but inquiry should be made during bad weather before attempting the latter route.

Bent's Old Fort — Located 13 km (8 miles) east of La Junta and 24 km (15 miles) west of Las Animas on Colorado 194.

Big Bend — Marfa, Texas to Presidio on U.S. 67, then State Road 170 to West Entrance (Maverick); State Road 118 from Alpine to the West Entrance; or U.S. 385 from Marathon to North Entrance (Persimmon Gap).

Big Thicket — The preserve units are scattered north and northeast of Beaumont, Texas, and can be reached from U.S. 69. Stop at the temporary preserve headquarters located at 6725 Eastex Freeway (U.S. 69) for orientation and a vicinity map.

Black Canyon of the Gunnison — Montrose, Colorado east via U.S. 50 for 10 km (6 miles), then 8 km (5 miles) north, hard surfaced road to South Rim entrance, open year round. From Colorado 92 just east of Crawford to North Rim, 23 km (14 miles) graded road, open only in summer.

Bryce Canyon — Usually entered from U.S. 89. At Bryce Junction, 11 km (7 miles) south of Panguitch, Utah, turn east on Utah 12, an all-paved road.

Canyon de Chelly — All-weather paved roads approach from Gallup, New Mexico via Window Rock, Ganado and Chinle; from Holbrook, or Keams Canyon, via Route 264 and Route 63 to Chinle; and from Kayenta via Mexican Water, Round Rock, and Many Farms, to Chinle.

Canyonlands — About 14.5 km (9 miles) north of Moab, on U.S. 163, a paved road takes off left, serving both Canyonlands and Dead Horse Point state park. Road paved to within about 10 km (6 miles) of Canyonlands, with good dirt roads entering area to all major points of interest.

About 56 km (35 miles) south of Moab and 27 km (17 miles) north of Monticello on U.S. 163 a paved road, Utah 211, proceeds west 56 km (35 miles) to the park's Needles District. There are about 14.5 km (9 miles) of paved road and many miles of jeep road in the District.

The Maze District (west side of the park) is wild and rugged, difficult to enter or travel in. Four-wheel drive vehicles required, and road conditions change rapidly. Do not attempt a Maze trip without first obtaining current information from the National Park Service.

Capitol Reef — the Park is 117 km (73 miles) southeast of Richfield and Sigurd, Utah on U-24. It is located 153 km (95 miles) southwest of Greenriver, Utah on U-24 which intersects U.S. 50 & I-6 19 km (twelve miles) west of Greenriver. In summer U-54, nearly all paved, and U-117, graded road, provide an added scenic approach from Bryce Canyon National Park.

Capulin Mountain — Entrance to this northeastern New Mexico area is on New Mexico 325. It is 11 km (7 miles) from the town of Folsom, and 4.8 km (3 miles) from Capulin (on U.S. 64 and 87), and 47 km (29 miles) from Raton. Open year-round, the road to the summit is sometimes closed for a few days at a time by snow.

Carlsbad Caverns — Arrive by paved highway 62-180 from Carlsbad, New Mexico 43 km (27 miles) northeast of (and) El Paso, Texas about 241 km (150 miles) west. Daily bus service is available from both cities.

Casa Grande Ruins — The Monument is about midway between Phoenix and Tucson, Arizona, 3.2 km (2 miles) north of Coolidge on Arizona 87. Coolidge has rail and bus connections.

Cedar Breaks — Northeast of Zion National Park, 37 km (23 miles) from Cedar City and 43 km (27 miles) from Long Valley Junction, Utah, via State Routes 14 and 143. From Panguitch, Utah and U.S. 89 over paved county road. Cedar City offers commuter air service from Salt Lake City and Las Vegas, Nevada.

Chaco Canyon — In northwestern New Mexico, the area is reached from north or south over *unpaved* State Route 57. This is rough "washboard" dirt road, but passable by passenger cars. When wet it is extremely slippery and sometimes impassable. State Route 57 is entered from the north at Blanco Trading post, 66 km (41 miles) southeast of Farmington on State 44. From Blanco, it is 48 km (30 miles) to Chaco Canyon. From the south State Route 57 is entered at Thoreau on I-40. It is 97 km (60 miles) to Chaco Canyon, 32 (20) of which are dirt.

If weather is questionable, we invite you to telephone for information on road conditions: Area code 505 786-5384.

Chamizal — Immediately west of the Cordoba Island Port of Entry, the Memorial is accessible from either Paisano Drive or Delta Drive in El Paso, Texas.

Chickasaw — Located on U.S. 177 just south of the center of Sulphur, Oklahoma. State Route 7 connects Sulphur with Interstate 35 near Davis, Oklahoma, about 113 km (70 miles) south of Oklahoma City. "The Point" and "Guy Sandy" areas are reached by separate marked roads, turning south off State Route 7 between Sulphur and Davis. "Buckhorn" area is reached by turning west off U.S. 177 10 km (6 miles) south of Sulphur. Interstate 35 connects with Route 7 near Davis.

Chiricahua — The single entrance, on the west side of the Monument, is reached by paved road from Willcox, 58 km (36 miles), or by paved road from Douglas, 113 km (70 miles).

Colorado — Paved highways and graded and surfaced roads available from all directions. The monument is 6.5 km (4 miles) west of Grand Junction, 5.6 km (3½ miles) south of Fruita. U.S. 6, 50, and I-70 lead to Grand Junction; U.S. 6, 50 and I-70 lead to Fruita.

Coronado — Located near the Mexican boundary, 8 km (5 miles) off Arizona 92 midway between the towns of Bisbee and Sierra Vista, in Montezuma Canyon.

Curecanti — Located between Gunnison and Montrose, Colorado, on U.S. Highway 50, can also be reached via Colorado Highway 92 from Delta and Hotchkiss, and Colorado Highway 149 from Lake City. The Elk Creek Visitor Center on Blue Mesa Lake, open May through September, is 26 km (16 miles) west of Gunnison. The Cimarron Information Station, open June through August, is 32 km (20 miles) east of Montrose.

Dinosaur — The Quarry site is 11 km (7 miles) by paved road north from Jensen, Utah (on U.S. Highway 40), in the extreme northeastern corner of the state.

Best way to view the canyon area is the 50 km (31 mile) drive, oiled road, to Harpers Corner from Monument Headquarters, 1.6 km (1 mile) east of Dinosaur, Colorado, on U.S. 40.

El Morro — 93 km (58 miles) southeast of Gallup, New Mexico, via New Mexico 32 and 53, and 69 km (43 miles) west of Grants via New Mexico 53, on all-weather roads.

Florissant Fossil Beds — Located south of the village of Florissant, which is 56 km (35 miles) west of Colorado Springs on U.S. 24. The visitor center is 4 km (2.5 miles) south of Florissant.

Fort Bowie — From Willcox on Interstate 10 drive 35 km (22 miles) south on Arizona 186 to graded road leading east into Apache Pass; from Bowie, also on Interstate 10, drive southerly 19 km (12 miles) on graded dirt road, then westerly into Apache Pass.

67

Fort Davis — Reached from U.S. 90, east from Valentine, Texas via routes 505-166; north from Marfa via 17 and from Alpine via 118; from route 290, south from Toyahvale via 17 and from Kent via 118.

Fort Larned — Located 10 km (6 miles) west of Larned, Kansas, on paved U.S. 156. From Interstate 70 the Fort is 80 km (50 miles) via U.S. 183 and 137 km (85 miles) via U.S. 156.

Fort Union — Take New Mexico Highway 477 west, off Interstate 25 (U.S. 85), 47 km (28 miles) northeast of Las Vegas, New Mexico.

Gila Cliff Dwellings — Located 71 km (44 miles) north of Silver City, New Mexico, the area is reached from Silver City via State Routes 35 and 15, all paved. In snow weather or for those who prefer less mountainous roads, Route 61 from San Lorenzo may be used.

Glen Canyon — May be reached by all-weather, paved U.S. Highway 89, 143 km (89 miles) east of Kanab, Utah, or 209 km (130 miles) north of Flagstaff, Arizona. Page is served by scheduled airline and bus service. There are airstrips at Bullfrog, Halls Crossing, Marble Canyon, and Page.

Golden Spike — North of Great Salt Lake and 48 km (30 miles) west of Brigham City, Utah. To reach the Site travel 37 km (23 miles) westward on Utah 83 to Promontory Junction; turn left and go 3.2 km (2 miles) to next junction; then turn right and go 8 km (5 miles).

Grand Canyon National Park — Paved highway from either Flagstaff or Williams brings you to South Rim in less than 2 hours, and airlines, bus lines and railroad serve both cities. Airlines serve Grand Canyon at airport 13 km (8 miles) south of the Park. Busses from Grand Canyon Village meet each flight and also serve the Village from Williams and Flagstaff. North Rim, 71 km (44 miles) by paved road from Jacob Lake, Arizona, is served by public transportation, from mid-June through August, by bus from Cedar City, Utah.

Grand Canyon National Park (Tuweep Unit) — Approaches not paved, but graded and kept in generally fair condition, although impassable for short periods after heavy storms. You arrive from Fredonia, Arizona, on U.S. 89A, 105 km (65 miles) distant; from Short Creek, Arizona, 88 km (55 miles) away and U.S. 91 from St. George, Utah, 145 km (90 miles) away, in summer. Via Fredonia and Short Creek there is no habitation until arrival at the N.P.S. Tuweep Ranger Station.

Gran Quivira — Leave U.S. 60 at Mountainair, New Mexico and go south on State Route 14 for 42 km (26 miles). Or, from Carrizozo go north and drive 90 km (56 miles) via U.S. 54 and State 14, unpaved for 63 km (39 miles). Or, in good weather, you may turn off U.S. 380 at Bingham and north on State 41.

Great Sand Dunes — Approach roads are Colorado 150 which leaves Colorado 160 8 km (five miles) west of Blanca, and a paved county road, which leaves Colorado 17 1.6 km (one mile) north of Mosca.

Guadalupe Mountains — The park entrance is adjacent to U.S. 62-180, some 88 km (55 miles) southwest of Carlsbad, New Mexico and 177 km (110 miles) east of El Paso, Texas. The New Mexico-Texas state line is the north boundary.

Hovenweep — Approach roads, from Routes 160 and 666, are gravel or graded dirt roads, normally passable to passenger cars except during or after severe storms. The road from the south via Aneth, Hatch Trading Post, and McElmo Canyon Road south of Cortez is now mostly gravelled. Call Mesa Verde 303-524-4434 for current road information.

Hubbell Trading Post — Immediately adjacent to Arizona State Highway 264, 1.6 km (one mile) west of Ganado, Arizona. All-weather roads lead from the four points of the compass.

Lake Mead — Various sections of this huge recreational area may be reached by good highways from Kingman, Arizona; Needles, California; and Las Vegas, Nevada. Inquire at the visitor center, 601 Nevada Highway, Boulder City, Nevada 89005 for information on how best to enjoy the area.

Lake Meredith — 56 km (35 miles) northeast of Amarillo, Texas, on State Highway 136, near the town of Fritch, is the recreation area. A few miles east, on the same highway, is Borger. The area is also reached by State 152 from Dalhart via Stinnett on the north. Access to the Rosita Area (for off-road vehicles) is from Highway 287 at the Canadian River bridge.

Lehman Caves — The Monument is 18 km (11 miles) south of U.S. Highway 6 and 50, and is reached by Nevada State Highways 73 and 74 via Baker, Nevada. Ely, Nevada, is 109 km (68 miles) to the west. Delta, Utah, is 166 km (103 miles) to the east on U.S. 6 and 50, while Milford, Utah, is 148 km (92 miles) southwest on Nevada 73 and Utah Highway 21.

Lyndon B. Johnson — The park is composed of the Birthplace and Boyhood Home Sites. The Birthplace is 3.2 km (two miles) east of Stonewall, Texas, on Park Road 49, and is reached from Ranch Road 1 just north of U.S. Highway 290, near the L.B.J. Ranch. The Boyhood Home is about 21 km (13 miles) east in Johnson City, one block south of U.S. 290. Both sites can be reached by using U.S. Highway 290. Park headquarters office is located in the U.S. Post Office building in Johnson City.

Mesa Verde — The park entrance is midway between Cortez and Mancos, Colorado, on U.S. 160, which connects with a number of major highways that approach the Park from all directions. From the entrance there is 34 km (21 miles) of all-weather mountainous road to Park headquarters and the major Park attractions.

Montezuma Castle — In the center of Arizona, turn east off Interstate 17 at the Montezuma Castle National Monument exit, to the Castle, 1.6 km (a mile) away, or the McGuireville-Page Springs exit, to the Well, 6.4 km (4 miles) away. From Cottonwood-Clarkdale-Jerome you go southeast on 279 to I-17, then north on I-17. From the Sedona area, you go south on 179 to I-17, then southeast on I-17.

Natural Bridges — 6.4 km (four miles) south of Blanding, Utah, on State Route 47, you leave the graded highway and turn west on State 95, an excellent paved road, for over 40 km (25 miles). The route is open all year long, and is a spectacular drive, as well as being the only east-west route across the Colorado River between Moab, Utah and Page, Arizona.

Navajo — To reach Monument headquarters you drive 88 km (55 miles) northeast of Tuba City, or 35 km (22 miles) southwestward from Kayenta, Arizona, both on State Highway 160 (Navajo Trail), then 14 km (9 miles) north on State Highway 564.

Organ Pipe Cactus — From Phoenix, take U.S. 80 to Gila Bend and then Arizona 85 south to the Monument. From Tucson, take Arizona 86 and then Arizona 85 south. From Mexicali, take Route 2 to Sonoyta, and then north.

Padre Island — The north end of the island is reached via State Highway 358 and Park Road 22 from Corpus Christi or via Park Road 53 from Port Aransas. The south end is accessible via State Highway 100 to Port Isabel. Both ends are connected to the mainland by county operated causeways. The 182 km (113 mile) long island parallels the east Texas coast and 129 km (80.3 miles) within the boundaries of the National Seashore. Travel along the length of the island is feasible with 4-wheel drive vehicles, but short trips at each end can be taken along beaches with standard passenger cars. The Mansfield boat channel cuts through the southern part of the area and prevents a continuing trip down the entire length. Many sections of the island can be reached by boats traveling down the Intra-Coastal Waterway.

Pecos — About 40 km (25 miles) southeast from Santa Fe, New Mexico, the Monument is easily accessible a few miles off Interstate 25 and Alternate U.S. 84-85. Visitor use facilities are presently being developed.

Petrified Forest — U.S. Highway 66 (Interstate 40), crossing the Park near the Painted Desert, is the approach from the east. Visitors from the west, southwest, and south should save mileage by entering via U.S. 180 from Holbrook. The Park road connects these two main highways.

Pipe Spring — 24 km (15 miles) southwest of Fredonia, Arizona, the area can be reached from US. 89 via Arizona 389. From U.S. 91, Utah 15 and 17 connect with Utah 59 at Hurricane, Utah, from which a paved road leads 66 km (41 miles) to the Monument.

Rainbow Bridge — It is 80 km (50 miles) by boat from the Wahweap Headquarters of Glen Canyon National Recreation Area in Arizona to the landing in Bridge Canyon, Utah. From the landing, it is approximately .4 km (¼ mile) by trail to Rainbow Bridge arch. By advance arrangement, it is possible to reach the Bridge by trail from Rainbow Lodge, 23 km (14 miles), or from Navajo Mountain Trading Post, 39 km (24 miles).

Rocky Mountain — Nearest major rail, air and busline terminals are at Denver, 105 km (65 miles) from Estes Park, and at Cheyenne, Wyoming, 146 km (91 miles) distant. Gray Line Tours connect with transcontinental airlines, railroads and buslines at Denver. A major network of fine highways reaches the area, including Route 34 from Greeley and points east, and several routes from Denver and Boulder. U.S. 40 and U.S. 34 approach the park through Granby and Grand Lake on the west.

Saguaro — The Rincon Mountain Section is easily reached from downtown Tucson by driving east on Broadway or 22nd Street to the